Paper Camera

Paper Camera
A Half Century with New Rivers Press

SUZZANNE KELLEY, EDITOR

ALICIA STRNAD HOALCRAFT, ASSISTANT EDITOR

Cover design by Renato de Araújo Gomes
Interior design by Daniel A. Shudlick and Michele F. Valenti

The publication of *Paper Camera: A Half Century with New Rivers Press* is made possible by the generous support of Minnesota State University Moorhead, the McKnight Foundation, the Dawson Family Fund, Lake Region Arts Council, Northern Lights Library Network, and other contributors to New Rivers Press.

This publication is funded in part by a grant from the Lake Region Arts Council through a Minnesota State Legislative appropriation.

For academic permission or copyright clearance, please contact
Frederick T. Courtright at 570-839-7477 or permdude@eclipse.net.

New Rivers Press is a nonprofit literary press associated with
Minnesota State University Moorhead.

Alan Davis, Co-Director and Senior Editor
Suzzanne Kelley, Co-Director and Managing Editor
Wayne Gudmundson, Consultant
Thom Tammaro, Poetry Editor
Kevin Carollo, MVP Poetry Coordinator

Publishing Interns: David Binkard, Katelin Hansen, Jan Hough, Kjersti Maday, Richard D. Natale, Emily Nelson, Joe Schneider, Daniel A. Shudlick, Lauren Stanislawski, Michele F. Valenti

Paper Camera: A Half Century with New Rivers Press Book Team:
Katie Baker, David Binkard, Emilee Ruhland, Lauren Stanislawski, and the 2014 Introduction to Publishing class: Jan Hough (Teaching Assistant), Marcus Amundson, Nathanael Bakke, Adam Barone, Chantz Block, Jalen Burchill, Madeline Cameron, Molly Christenson, Grant Evans, Benjamin Friesen, Meagan Gaughan, Moriah Hamstad, Emily Jetvig, Hannah Kiges, Morgan Laite, Kirsten Lusty, Kjersti Maday, Kristin Miller, Joseph Overmoe, Zana Pommier, Austin Rau, Jessica Steinke, Carrie Thayer

Printed in the United States of America
Distributed nationally by Small Press Distribution

New Rivers Press
c/o MSUM
1104 7th Avenue South
Moorhead, MN 56563
newriverspress.com

This anthology is dedicated to the students, writers, editors, and patrons of independent press publishing, "where the ink is pressed deep."

—quote from "The Paper Camera," by Joyce Sutphen

CONTENTS

DYNAMIC RANGE

Alicia Strnad Hoalcraft, a recent graduate of Minnesota State University Moorhead, is now a nationally recognized News Page Designer at The Forum of Fargo-Moorhead. While completing her Certificate in Publishing, she was a member of the New Rivers Press book team for Haints, *by Clint McCown.*

From the Assistant Editor

I joined New Rivers Press in fall 2011 as a student in the Practicum in Publishing course. In the class, one of my favorites I took during my years of college, I was a member of the book team for Clint McCown's award-winning novel, *Haints.* Team editing that book is still one of my best college experiences, so when New Rivers Press Managing Editor Suzzanne Kelley asked me to consider joining the New Rivers team as an intern the next semester, I jumped at the chance.

When I got to the office for my internship, Suzzanne presented me with a fairly straightforward task: Compile all the articles used as teaching material in the Introduction to Publishing class, get copyright permissions, and turn the articles into a book for students to use in that class in future years. It wasn't long, however, before I discovered it wasn't feasible to do what I was asked—just getting the permissions for the first week's readings would cost more than New Rivers could afford for the entire book.

I told Suzzanne that I wouldn't be able to do what she'd asked of me, unsure what this would mean for my internship. We were both disappointed that we wouldn't be able to produce the volume. I don't remember who mentioned it first, but while discussing the only article the press could afford to print—Bill Truesdale's contribution to the New Rivers Press anthology *The Talking of Hands* (his article is reprinted in this volume)—we realized 2013 marked not only New Rivers Press's 45th year of publishing, but also the 10th year since the press moved to Minnesota State University Moorhead, and the university's 125th year. "Wouldn't it be nice," Suzzanne mused, "to do something to mark that occasion?"

By the end of the conversation, the idea was born to contact people who had been a part of New Rivers over the years—authors, administrators, interns, and others—and have them write a piece about their experiences with the press and compile them into an anthology to celebrate the history of New Rivers Press. I spent the next several months corresponding with various people connected with the press, soliciting submissions, then compiling and editing them before turning them over to Suzzanne. The project extended past the end of my internship and past my graduation from MSUM.

My experience with New Rivers Press extended past the courses I took, but it's very similar to that shared by students who complete the Certificate in Publishing program. While students in other programs have a transcript or class project to show for their efforts, students who complete the publishing coursework get to hold a published book with their name in it, something they can show to future employers (or, like I did, give to their mothers as a Christmas present).

As described in the contributions to this anthology, New Rivers Press is a small press unlike any other, and its contributions to its authors and students—and to others connected to it—are many. This anthology represents the experiences of a small percentage of the people who have helped shape New Rivers over the past half century, and I am proud to say I am now a part of the history of this organization.

SUZZANNE KELLEY

Suzzanne Kelley has worked as managing editor and co-director for New Rivers Press since the fall of 2009. She has directed the publication of more than forty books of scholarly and literary nonfiction, fiction, and poetry. Kelley also researches and writes about memory and rural life in the Great Plains, New Zealand, and Australia.

From the Editor

Welcome to our New Rivers Press celebration anthology. As Alicia, the assistant editor to this collection of essays described, *Paper Camera: A Half Century with New Rivers Press* originated with the need for a text in our Introduction to Publishing class as well as a celebration of our rare longevity. Our intention was to provide students and interns with a general knowledge of the history of New Rivers, but also a working knowledge of the publishing field. Our plans grew, however, to be more encompassing of the field. In the selection of authors and their narratives, we found a larger story gently unfolding. Writers, many of them experiencing for the first time the thrill (and angst) of seeing their manuscripts take the form of a published book, told the story of how they came to be published authors. Board members and interns wrote of their investment in New Rivers Press, sometimes monetary, but always philosophical and artistic. Students, who also experienced the publishing world for the first time, shared the insights they gleaned as they completed real projects—books, with academic and editorial credits—that they could carry away from Minnesota State University Moorhead upon graduation. Some of our students have gone on to their own publishing ventures—some working as far away as New York and New Jersey, and two beginning their own start-up publishing companies right here in the Fargo-Moorhead area.

Alicia's experience, just as she laid it out in her introductory comments, exemplifies the New Rivers Press dual mission: to publish enduring contemporary literature by new, emerging, and established authors and to provide learning opportunities for all kinds of students, matriculating and otherwise. Alicia began with a project, tailored to expand skills she already had, while venturing out into something brand new and at the same time contributing to the mission and promotion of New

Rivers Press. She dove into the project with zeal. Before long she delivered to me a prospectus, a sample table of contents, and a list—which we together contrived—of people to contact for possible contributions to our anthology. And then she began writing letters and making phone calls. Her efforts and her well-reasoned plans earned her real recognition for her work: her name on the front cover. And then she graduated. And then she married. And then she had baby Callie. Our book has been a long time coming, and life has gone on in its many directions with just as many distractions from the work at hand. But like others who invested in New Rivers Press, Alicia is seeing the job through to its end.

For the longest time, we had no name for our anthology. When we'd sit at the conference table in the office with interns Katie Baker and Emilee Ruhland, who had early hands in editing, the four of us would refer to the developing anniversary manuscript as Annibook. It wasn't until our involvement in a collaborative project on campus that the title, *Paper Camera*, came to mind. New Rivers Press commissioned Minnesota Poet Laureate Joyce Sutphen to write an original poem, while the Art Department commissioned a letterprint artist, Margot Ecke (of Athens, Georgia) to design a broadside. When I say we "commissioned" Joyce to produce her poems, I have to elaborate that the amount of the commission was more like an honorarium, nay, more like a token, and we are forever grateful that she cared to join us in our project. Joyce was most generous with her time and talent: Instead of one poem, she sent to us, as she described it, a "sheaf" of poems—ten in number! One of them, "The Paper Camera," practically announced itself as the best title for our anthology, and we believe you will agree as you follow its lines and follow us to where "the ink is pressed deep." (See p. 3).

In the past year, as Alicia, Emilee, and Katie moved on, two more interns joined the *Paper Camera* book team: David Binkard and Lauren Stanislawski. Over the months, new (and not-so-new) authors were asked to contribute, even beyond the core list that Alicia solicited. Dave and Lauren compiled all of the essays, began copyediting, and assisted in collating the essays into a timeline, or perhaps better said, a storyline. Our story begins with Bill Truesdale telling us the history of the press he founded, and then the narrative ambles into different perspectives from authors and board members who were among the first to experience Bill's editorial hand. From a founder-driven press to a teaching press, the collection of essays illustrates a press in a constant mode of development, angling for new and better frames within which we might accomplish our mission, sending out snapshots of history over a period of nearly fifty years, and producing a panoramic picture of New Rivers Press.

Chronology of New Rivers Press

1968
New Rivers Press is established in New York by C.W. Truesdale to publish new and emerging poets. Later, fiction and nonfiction are added.

1978
New Rivers moves to a location on Selby Avenue in St. Paul, Minnesota.

1981
The Minnesota Voices Project, a literary competition for unpublished and newly emerging writers, is established.

1982
New Rivers Press obtains 501(c)3 nonprofit status.

1984
The Many Minnesotas Project, a series of writing from ethnic groups in Minnesota is established. In addition, New Rivers Abroad becomes the series title for translations of literary writing from outside the United States.

1989
New Rivers Press moves to the Ford Centre in Minneapolis. A managing editor is hired who contributes to grant writing. This is New Rivers Press's second employee. Two years later, a third employee is added.

1996
Consortium Books Sales and Distribution, the premier distributor for small literary presses in the United States, signs a contract with New Rivers to sell its books. David Haynes, author of two New Rivers Press books, *Right by My Side* and *Heathens*, is chosen by *Granta* as one of

the Best Young American Novelists Under Forty in 1997. A collaboration of the five literary presses of Minnesota receives funding from the Star Tribune Foundation to hire a subsidiary rights agent to sell paperback, film, and foreign rights.

1998
New Rivers Press celebrates its 30th anniversary. C.W. Truesdale receives the Kay Sexton Award for contributions to the community of the book. The anthology *Tanzania on Tuesday* receives a Minnesota Book Award. The first book of prose poetry in the Marie Alexander series is *Traffic*, by New Yorker Jack Anderson.

1999
The Talking of Hands wins the Minnesota Book Award. *A Degree of Mastery* by Annie Tremmel Wilcox is chosen as an alternate by the Book-of-the-Month Club, and paperback rights are sold to Penguin. C.W. Truesdale steps down as publisher. Robert Alexander is chosen Creative Director. New Rivers Press receives a grant from the NEA for Southeast Asian American Writing: *Tilting the Continent*.

2000
New Rivers Press moves its offices to Suite 1180 in the Ford Centre. The 100th book in Minnesota Voices Project is published.

2001
New Rivers Press relocates to Minnesota State University Moorhead. It agrees to publish existing books under contract.

2003-Present
New Rivers Press publishes its first three titles under its new arrangement. It now has a dual mission: to acquire, publish, and promote the most enduring contemporary literature that it can find and to provide academic learning opportunities for students. A certificate in publishing is available for students. Besides the MVP Series, New Rivers Press at MSUM has partnered with The Plains Art Museum to publish a gallery catalog and reappraisal of the sculptor Duane Hanson, with the Stonecoast MFA Program to publish the winner of the Stonecoast Book Prize, and with Fairfield University to publish the Fairfield Book Prize. We actively seek such partnerships.

Exposure

JOYCE SUTPHEN

Joyce Sutphen, Minnesota's poet laureate, contributed ten previously unpublished poems for this publication, including "The Paper Camera." Sutphen worked previously with New Rivers Press as co-editor for To Sing Along the Way: Minnesota Women Poets from Pre-Territorial Days to the Present *(2006).*

The Paper Camera

Someone should invent
a paper camera,

and we could all live
happily ever after

on a page where
the ink is pressed deep

into the words you
are reading now—

words that tell us
how sweet

it was to be alive
in the days of print

and how easy it was
to say "sparrow"

even in the middle
of winter.

C.W. "BILL" TRUESDALE

C.W. "Bill" Truesdale was the founder and longtime editor of New Rivers Press, Minnesota's oldest nonprofit publisher. Known as a risk-taker, he helped to launch scores of previously-unknown literary authors such as poet Charles Simic and Minnesotans David Haynes and Charles Baxter. Truesdale wrote the following essay at the celebration of New Rivers Press's thirtieth anniversary. This essay first appeared in The Talking of Hands *(1998).*

New Rivers Press:
A History (1968-98)

*T*hose of us who began publishing in the small press literary field in the sixties were likely to be naïve, sometimes idealistic, often governed by vanity, and full of illusions about what we were setting out to accomplish.

New Rivers Press was no exception. Even though I was nearly forty years old when I started it in Nyack, New York, in February 1968, it was a wholly new and exhilarating experience for me. I had, by then, been a full-time college professor for more than thirteen years, had a PhD in English and Comparative Literature (which I received from the University of Washington in Seattle in 1956), was married and had three children, and had three books of my own poetry published (the first in Mexico City, the second in Denver, and the third in New York City). The only previous experience I'd had with any small press was with El Corno Emplumado, run by Margaret Randall and Sergio Mondragón in Mexico City (my first publishers). The fact that I was by then a very active and committed poet made me much like almost all of my compatriots in the small press field. And like most of them, too, I was strongly opposed to the Vietnam War (though my older brother, John, served there as a major in the Green Berets in 1965-66). Also like most of them, I had no idea what I was getting myself into. I didn't even know in the beginning that there were hundreds of other small presses and literary magazines being thrown together all over America at that time—that, indeed, a kind of Renaissance was taking place in this country, a literary explosion that lasted well into the seventies.

Unlike many small press publishers in the sixties, I did not start my own press for any political reason, even though most of the books I was to publish over the next dozen or so years had a strong political basis. Primarily, I was motivated by two things: 1) My background was in the centuries-long practice of great literature in England. As a teacher my specialty had been, of all unlikely things, medieval literature—Chaucer, Langland, the Pearl Poet, and the medieval romance—but I was well-acquainted with other major periods and authors as well. 2) I'd had one hell of a time getting my own first book published. I was thirty-seven years old when my first book came out, and I wanted to make it just a little bit easier for other first book authors to get their poetry published, a motivation that still characterizes the mission of New Rivers Press.

Starting New Rivers was not something I set out deliberately to do. Ever since I'd been in Mexico two years before and had observed El Corno Emplumado, I had, to be sure, dreamed of starting a similar, though less political, press in the United States. After I left full-time teaching in the spring of 1967, I did talk a lot about something like that, but I didn't do anything about it—not until my late ex-brother-in-law, Bill Chaffee (an architect who worked for I.M. Pei in New York City), bought a farm near Southfield, Massachusetts, in late 1967. Bill told me there was an old letterpress sitting in a shed near his new old house and that I could certainly have it if I really wanted to put my feet where my mouth had been for so long. Otherwise, he was just going to have to get rid of it. At that time, I knew nothing about printing, had never heard of letterpresses or offset lithography, and had certainly never even thought about actually getting involved in printing.

But, being my father's son, I swallowed that particular hook. I went up to Southfield to look over the situation and what I saw was an old-fashioned Chandler & Price letterpress that had not been used for years. George, the son of the previous owners of the place (from whom he had inherited the farm as well as this old monster of a machine), told me all about what it had been used for. The shed where it was located had been a Christmas card factory of sorts. The cards themselves had been silkscreened and the press had been used to print Christmas sentiments inside the folded-over cards.

The press itself was something of a mess. The basic mechanism—a huge flywheel that closed the two gigantic maws like a clamshell—was intact, there were a couple of chases (for holding the handset type in place), but the inking mechanism had been disconnected and scattered all over the place, and the suction cups that lifted the paper were in pathetic shape. But George said I would find it a breeze to print. He showed me the instruction book that came with the press, and it seemed reasonable and simple enough that I could master printing in no time flat. I left Massachusetts a little drunk (from exhilaration, yes, and also from bourbon) and resolved to go up there in a month or two and start the actual printing of what became the first three New Rivers books. I knew myself well enough, however, to figure out that I had no intention of setting type by hand.

I soon found a printer in West Nyack (about ten miles from where I lived) who had an old linotype machine and—more importantly—a guy named Jim who knew how to use it. He was fairly young for a profession that was rapidly disappearing. I had him set the first two books on that machine and bought what I hoped would be enough paper to start printing. All of which—the lead slugs, which must have weighed a thousand pounds, for two small books, as well as the boxes of very expensive and rather elegant stock, and the clothes and other stuff I would need—I loaded up in my Volvo.

When I got to Southfield and found my way back to the farm, not only George but that Chandler & Price instruction manual had disappeared. I really knew nothing at all about printing and was thus faced with what I can only call a true existential experience. The nearest help was miles and miles away, and, besides, I was just too crazy with pride to admit I needed help.

February in Massachusetts is not like February in Minnesota but it was certainly cold enough. Cold enough for snowmobiles (a relatively new invention at that time) to roar past on those country and very much unplowed roads. The house, which Bill and Connie Chaffee had completely remodeled, was certainly warm enough, but that shed was heated by a small, inefficient oil heater. It took an hour or more to heat up the place—and the printing ink, which I rapidly discovered had an aversion to cold weather.

Heat—or the lack of it—turned out to be the least of my problems. I found out almost immediately that there was no way I could get the automatic inking device on the press to work (I couldn't even figure out how to put it together). This meant I had to hand ink the press, which, in turn, meant that every page I managed to print came out different from all the others, so that the inking throughout both of those two books, especially the first one, was inconsistent and, frankly, a total mess. Since the press was too small to print more than two pages at a time, this inconsistency became very noticeable.

Furthermore, I could never get the feeding device to work properly and had to hand feed each sheet of stock, which meant sticking my right hand between those two great maws before they could close and mangle it. It also took me a long time to figure out how to make each lead slug in the chase come out clearly. After trial and error, I discovered that using little strips of paper underneath some of the slugs did the job well enough. What this meant was that I had to spend at least fifteen or twenty minutes preparing every two pages in the whole book. This wasn't a problem with the first two books because they were no more than twenty-five pages in length. But it became a real hassle with the third book (Al Greenberg's *The Metaphysical Giraffe*), because it was somewhere around seventy pages in length.

The third New Rivers book presented yet another problem. Lead printing slugs are about four inches wide. Al's lines were often no more than an inch to an inch and a half in width. When I tried to print this book, I found that the ends of each slug marked the page with blobs of ink. The only way I could correct this problem was to trim down the ends of each slug with a power saw (which, fortunately, that shed possessed). This certainly corrected the problem of the slugs, but it also meant, since it was now very warm in the shed, that I sprayed my left arm with lead pellets and nicked it constantly. It's a wonder I didn't come down with a bad case of lead-poisoning! It took me most of the summer just to print that third book.

The Metaphysical Giraffe was the very last book I printed in Massachusetts. Not only was I spending an enormous amount of time up there, but I also found that it was costing me far more than I had imagined, even just for the stock alone. I was spending at least three times as much for that paper as an ordinary printer would because such a printer buys it in huge quantities and hence gets a large discount. It would be much cheaper to have New Rivers books printed by offset lithography even if I hadn't been spending an inordinate amount of precious time doing the actual printing. I could spend far less time and money bringing out more and more books each year, and I could do the things like editing and writing that I had much more talent for.

Still, I did learn a great deal about printing—the hard way—a knowledge that makes me appreciate printing technology all that much more. Besides, I have a real respect for people doing physical things with their hands. I've never liked having people do things for me—perhaps that's kind of a reverse snobbism on my part. Even in my first marriage (when we had plenty of money), I did most of the things on our farm (near Lexington, Virginia) that had to be done— brushhogging the pastures, putting in fields of alfalfa, doing most of the carpentry work on the ancient barn, and even, when necessary, shoeing our horses.

***

One of the things I did learn in Southfield during the six months or so I did my own printing there was that I had no particular interest in the art of fine printing itself. I've always loved beautiful books as objects but I knew only too well that such objects were, for most people who bought them at very high prices, simply objects that were seldom if ever actually read. My own interest lay in the book itself and what it had to say or what it actually created.

What really concerned me from the beginning was the character of the writing, something that, for better or worse, reflected my own taste and judgment as a writer and as a publisher. Thus, though I started New Rivers in the midst of the darkest days of the Vietnam War and was under considerable pressure to publish anti-war books, I always resisted that impulse. From the first, I wanted to publish the very best books by new writers I could find, regardless of their political and social correctness. Although almost all of the writers I published shared my own antagonism toward that war, that wasn't the reason I published them, any more than, nowadays, I am driven to make editorial judgments by multiculturalism or any other current fashion. What interested me then and still very much does is the quality and originality of individual writing voices. For instance, I knew very well from my own background in reading and writing that English and American authors had produced very little in the way of effective poetry with strong political convictions. In all the many centuries of English literature I knew of only a handful of really first-rate political poems. This is probably not true of other cultures—like those of the countries that used to be dominated by the then-Soviet Union, or some of the formerly colonial territories once dominated by the imperial powers. Most of the political manuscripts that came to me in the early years of New Rivers were strident, impersonal, and likely to be manifesto-type utterances.

To say, however, that I was not interested in manuscripts that, at least sometimes, were politically oriented would be misleading. I knew very well that really good writing sometimes reflected strong political engagement and was a way for writers to cope with the social and political issues of the day, and that some of the very best writing came about because the writer was deeply disturbed or even traumatized by such crises as the Vietnam War or by the prevailing conservatism of the American public, or by the growing violence in our urban centers. Often enough, these writers saw that deep social issues were reflected in their personal lives. I could not myself write directly about the Vietnam War until my brother went over there as a Green Beret.

In that sense, then, many of the writers I was to publish in the first decade of New Rivers' history were very much politically engaged. Not all of them were activists by any means and none of them, so far as I knew, wrote anything like a political manifesto. Few, if any, had anything like final answers. What interested me in them as writers was the character and individuality of their responses and their take on the country they had been brought up in.

Similarly, these days—when the Vietnam War has long been over—I don't pay much mind to the renewed interested in formalist poetry. It runs very much against the grain of what I consider the best American poetry of the twentieth century, much of which derives from free verse techniques first introduced by Walt Whitman, who remains an abiding influence on our poetry. That formalism has always been much more at home in England I certainly appreciate. In fact, one of the very best poets in English in this century is, to me, William Butler Yeats, and he regularly used distinct forms and rhyme. I am not philosophically adverse to formalism per se. I just don't happen to believe that it usually works in American poetry—with rare exceptions. (I have even published a few American formalists simply because that way of writing is best for them. The work of Charles Molesworth, whose *Common Elegies* I published many years ago, immediately comes to mind.)

Because my interest in new writing and highly individual voices has always been paramount to me, and insofar as New Rivers has always reflected my own taste and judgment, this press has never been associated with any particular school of writing—Black Mountain, New York, L.A.N.G.U.A.G.E., Ethno- or Mytho-Poetic, or, today, Hyper-Text—even though I have occasionally published writers who have been affiliated with one group or another. For this reason, New Rivers has often been called "eclectic." Eclecticism is not a negative term as far as I am concerned—so long as that word does not imply absence of taste or slackness of editorial judgment. In my view, every book that New Rivers brings out is like no other book ever published—the last thing in the world I would like New Rivers Press to be seen as doing is publishing clones of my own work as a writer. Really first-rate writing is always unique to the author, never standard.

***

When I think of New Rivers in general terms, as I am doing here, I think of the many, many different voices we have published in individual books and anthologies over the years, and of the enormous variety of subjects that these authors—including those who live in this immediate area and have been published in our Minnesota Voices Project—give unique voice to, and of what American literature would be like without them. Our culture would be very much diminished, I fear, because I know very well how hard it is to get books published these days, particularly those by new authors (whatever their age might be). Many of these authors would probably have given up on the idea of ever being published at all, if New Rivers had not been around to help them gain recognition.

When I think of all of those authors—and of many we simply could not publish—I am just amazed at the depth and variety of writing, and I am very proud that New Rivers has been able to publish as much as we have.

I wrote an essay called "Aire and Angells: Poems About Writing Poetry" that was published in *The North Dakota Quarterly* in the Spring of 1988. Poems written about poetry don't usually interest me in the least (they strike me as being claustrophobic or self-indulgent) but there have been some very great exceptions in English and American literature—poems by John Donne, George Herbert, John Keats, and William Butler Yeats, among others. In that essay, I talked a great deal about editing and my relationship with authors, one of whom, Catherine Stearns, I used as an example of someone who had written an extraordinarily fine poem about writing poetry.

Among other things, I said, "More often than not I don't know these writers or know them only casually. But, because of the way the manuscripts are selected and because of my involvement in the process, I already know them very well on a level which counts very much to me—their work. I make it a practice to conduct meetings as casually as possible because there is a lot of potential fear and awe there, particularly for new writers, as most of them are. It's important for me to get to know them on a friendly, non-intimidating basis, because I want them to concentrate on their work and not on the ultimate fact of publication. Awe can be amusing enough, especially when it is coupled with the rather large egomania that often accompanies the acceptance of a first book, but it is not at all a creative emotion. Shaping a book requires tough, intelligent, objective work on the part of both author and editor. It is important for me to earn the respect of the authors I deal so often with, to establish a confidence in them that I can be of help or service to them. I want them to know that I have their best interests as writers at heart and that I can bring a good deal of experience and critical intelligence to this work.

"I enjoy doing this very much, and basically love working with writers on a creative basis—even if it is sometimes exhausting and very time-consuming. My life has become a complex series of dramatic encounters with some of the most interesting persons in the world. These take place in a structured way and on more basic levels than in ordinary associations, as in therapy, but there the resemblance ends. My role is more or less fixed, but the resulting play of minds and dance of spirits is anything but fixed. And it is rewarding too—both for the author who is likely to get a stronger book out of the process, and for me because stronger books make me look better as a publisher and because it's nice to have the power to be able to influence someone else in positive ways."

What I said of Stearns' poem at the end of that essay applies, I think, to just about any first-rate writer I have ever published: "In writing beautifully about a simple, very private experience, she gives her own voice and substance mythic dimensions, which is what all true poetry does. In doing this, she gives us a rare glimpse into a process that is at once real and tangible but also visionary and transcendent—familiar and ordinary as a doorway, strange and mysterious as a threshold."

C.W. "Bill" Truesdale, from the cover of *Doctor Vertigo* (wyrd press, 1975)

JOYCE SUTPHEN

At Home

Then I knew it was true,
that I was one of them,
that we were born speaking
the same language, and that
language was our only home.

So then I knew we could be
at ease with each other,
that none of us would care
if someone broke into blossom
or stormed the blank walls.

It was good to be at home
in the world for a minute
to find myself in the
background, playing bass,
just riffing on the melody.

CHARLES BAXTER

Charles Baxter has won numerous national awards for his books of non-fiction, poetry, edited works, and fiction, including The Feast of Love, *which was a finalist for the National Book Award and released as a movie starring Morgan Freeman. His first book,* Chameleon, *was published by New Rivers Press in 1970.*

An Emergency Meditation: Bill Truesdale and New Rivers Press

If you went into Calvin William Truesdale's office at Macalester College in April 1967, as I did, the first face you would have seen was a cartoon of Benjamin Franklin. This caricature-portrait of the founding father had been torn from the cover of *The Evergreen Review* and taped to the wall. *The Evergreen Review* was a sort of hipster leftist glossy magazine from that era; anyone who was paying attention to what was going on read it from cover to cover. In this cartoon, Franklin looked like a sly, shrewd, semi-criminal pragmatic joker with whom you wouldn't entrust a dime of your life savings. Nor would you trust him to babysit your daughter. Months or years later, I asked Bill why he had affixed Ben Franklin's portrait to his office wall. "I hate him," he said calmly.

Bill didn't like pragmatism. He wasn't even on the side of practicality. He didn't like shrewdness very much either, or careerism, or social climbing. And he didn't *look* shrewd. He was a large man, around six feet tall, with a prominent belly and long hair that he swept back from a wide credulous face. In those days his countenance broke into easygoing grins, but his customary expression was one of pensive inward contemplation, as if he had been permanently wounded by something. The wound kept him busy; he needed, it seemed, to find its source. As a result, he wasn't a particularly good observer. He had no distance on anything. He laughed easily, but he had a habit that persisted to the end of his life of interrupting you in the middle of your sentences as if you weren't there. These interruptions came from a voice that was at least one octave higher than you would have expected from a man of his size, and its tone was quizzical: a *mezzo-forte* hoarse tenor coming out of a bass-baritone body. His mouth was usually one-half or one-quarter open as if he couldn't breathe or had recently been starved.

He chain-smoked cigars, which he gave up for extended-length 120 millimeter cigarettes, the brand name for which was "More."

The first whiskey I ever drank, I got from him. That summer of 1967, he invited me over to the St. Paul house where he and his wife, Joan, lived with their three children. Seated in the living room, he asked me what liquor I preferred, and I said, "I don't know." I tried to be polite. "Anything."

"How about an Old Fashioned?" he asked.

"Fine," I said, having no idea what an Old Fashioned was. Wearing his Hush Puppy shoes, a plaid shirt, and khakis, Bill lumbered over to the liquor cabinet and began to pour out the bourbon and the bitters and the sugar water and the ice. Generosity constituted his first virtue. After my initial drink, which went down easily, the sun blazed in genial fashion through the west windows. Alvin Greenberg was there, talking about his recent Fulbright stay in India. Other people came and went.

After my second or third drink, I dimly perceived that Bill was saying that he and Joan were leaving St. Paul and going to live somewhere near New York City. Or was it Southfield, Massachusetts? He had bought a letterpress or was about to buy one. He would operate it. In one of his innumerable and lifelong Don Quixote gestures, Bill had also resigned from Macalester. I still have his enraged statement, printed up on a ditto machine, which he addressed to the Macalester student body. When he had arrived at Macalester, he wrote, "education itself was conceived of in broad, flexible, and meaningful terms." But *things had changed*.

"Respectability" was now the rage, "measured in numerical terms." Bill didn't like respectability. Officials had taken over, authority figures, father-types. Power-mad academics had been put in charge. (I am now paraphrasing.) Creeps with PhDs were calling the shots.

Bill himself had a PhD from the University of Washington, where he had known Theodore Roethke, but in his enraged statement one can discern the Truesdale passion for the underdog and the unofficial and the impulsive and the spontaneous and the local. This passion, along with his generosity, would serve as the foundation stones for New Rivers Press.

Anyway, he and Joan and their kids left Minnesota, though not before taking me up north to their cabin on Moccasin Lake, near Ely. I was a shy, self-conscious, twenty-year-old poet. That was enough. Bill and Joan overwhelmed me with kindness. The cabin had no running water, though it did have a propane stove and refrigerator, along with copious quantities of bourbon and other forms of solid and liquid bonhomie. However beautiful it was, the surrounding landscape was inward-looking and by no means benevolent. You would sit on the deck, reading your book and occasionally looking out at the lake where you had been swimming and where fish were now jumping at the surface, creating an echoing *thwap*, and in that terrible peace and quiet you would think your soul had somehow arisen and become visible to you, sometimes quite unpleasantly. The place was haunted by spirits. Many visitors thought so. Bill loved how remote it was.

He told me about a stream that went out of Moccasin Lake into another lake—Burntside, I think. To see it, one had to portage the canoe down this undergrowth-ridden stream, and we did that in 1967 or 1968 (I almost broke my leg on that portage), whereupon he wrote a poem about our excursion, a poem that had the idea of "new rivers" in it: discoveries, that is. The whole business of rivers seemed like a living metaphor to him; *The Loss of Rivers* (the title of his first book of poems) was like a death, a heart attack. I think he felt imprisoned much of the time—he wrote a book-length poem about Robert Stroud, the birdman of Alcatraz—and he was constantly seeking to discover ways and means to increase the blood flow, to bust out, to *circulate*, and this slightly manic urge to escape the confines of every limit and boundary ended up defining much of what he did.

I sent him my fledgling poems, about which he was generous and discerning despite their uneven awfulness (they had a few rare bursts of quality when their subject-matter was repression), and I saw him again during the following summers. Like a man in jail who'd become a demon correspondent, he sent long speculative letters, signed "Clyde" or "Fiddle," in the late 1960s about his work with the infernal letterpress he had bought. It was a big old thing, and it's a wonder he didn't injure himself with it more than he did. He wrote about this letterpress in his poem "The Heart of New Rivers Printing," from 1968. Here is an excerpt:

> a thousand leaden pounds of nonsense
> two hundred pounds of super-stock
> a nearly worthless mailing list
> a dozen moonward poems
> and other ditties of no tune
> it was existential
> that ascent into nothing
> new openings beginnings exhilarations
> "I can do anything!" I cried.

He *could* be ironic about his grandiosity. Then he and Joan moved to New York, to 215 West 92nd Street, and he moved the letterpress to Brooklyn, I think. I visited the Truesdales on West 92nd in early 1970. Somebody named Charles Simic dropped by, and he and Bill talked about Native Americans of whom I knew nothing. They also discussed a poet named Ivan V. Lalić, ditto, whom they were translating, or at least Simic was; Bill never learned Serbian, I don't think, though their translation of Lalić's poetry, *Fire Gardens*, was listed as a co-translation. The first New Rivers Press book that I do remember seeing was Alvin Greenberg's *The Metaphysical Giraffe* (I still own it), which Bill published in 1968 or 1969; it's copyrighted 1968, though I remember that it was delayed. The paper is brown stock, there is no title or author name on the spine, and the print is unevenly inked, though the witty and grotesque illustrations by Gene Roberds were printed on interpolated white pages. Bill printed it himself, as I remember. The poems themselves skinny-dipped down the page in narrow meditative stanzas. Witty, affectionate, grotesque, and indeed metaphysical, they were as unlike Bill's own work as could be. If there was to be a New Rivers aesthetic—I had always assumed that Whitman, Roethke, and Charles Olson would be the guiding forces, the expansive Big Breath guys—you couldn't find that aesthetic in Alvin Greenberg's poems. Which meant that the press was all about discoveries and not a particular aesthetic stance.

The Metaphysical Giraffe, by Alvin Greenberg (New Rivers Press, 1968), cover and drawings by Gene Robards

I have here in front of me an order form for New Rivers Press books from 1970. Al Greenberg's book is not listed, but among the ten books advertised, the first ten published by New Rivers, you can find Margaret Randall's leftist *So Many Rooms Has a House But One Roof*, listed price one dollar; a volume of Neruda's early poems translated by David Ossman, who was also a member of The Firesign Theater comedy group; the Simic-Truesdale translation of Ivan Lalić; Halvard Johnson's *Transparencies and Projections*; David Curry's *Here*; a volume of poems by Robin Fulton; another by John Knoepfle with slightly obscene illustrations; and one by me, *Chameleon*, copyright 1970, my first book.

I don't list that book among my publications anymore. I don't even like to think about it, and no force on Earth could induce me to reread it. But *Chameleon* kept me alive as a writer for a while, as did my second New Rivers Press book, *The South Dakota Guidebook*, published in 1974, both of them stalwart examples of early '70s surrealism. The other books he published, the Neruda and Randall books being exceptions, were mostly written in a mode of quietly enraged brainy lyricism salted with irony. That was the tone of most early New Rivers books, partly because that particular music was in the air as a consequence of the Vietnam War and cultural madness and manners, and partly because

Bill liked it. He liked my poems because they were so weird, and the wit in them was so desolate, and I think he believed that desolation in the face of empire building was a form of revolutionary preparedness.

If Bill turned his awareness toward you, and you were in need of a listener or someone who cared, he could save your life, given his open-handedness and bigheartedness. He gave me hospitality, food, booze, *attention*. When nobody much paid any notice, he did.

There were other recipients of that attention. Halvard Johnson's poetry, then and now, specialized in a kind of blocked-off narrative—Hal particularly liked shadowy mini-fables that ended not with enlightenment but puzzlement—and Hal's first book, *Transparencies and Projections*, was followed in rapid order by *The Dance of the Red Swan* and *Winter Journey*, a book to which I am tremendously indebted. I know that James Wright called up Bill to tell him that in Halvard Johnson, Bill had discovered "a real voice." I felt that Bill had indeed discovered a remarkable poet in Hal, and I felt the same way when he published Robin Fulton's translations of Lars Gustafsson. Those poems, with their urbane passionate melancholy and effortless learning, were like nothing else I had ever read. Bill's sense of taste was not impeccable, of course. There were duds. There always are. But he published Simic's great poem *White* (full of misprints) in 1972, when almost no one knew who Charles Simic was. Now, in 2012, as I write, everyone in the world who reads poetry knows about Charles Simic. In those days, before he was taken up by New Directions, no one knew who Lars Gustafsson was, either. By now, everyone should.

Probably the greatest of these early books was *Fire Gardens*, published in 1970, a collection of poems that Bill and Charles Simic co-translated. Lalić wrote in a style of "sensual and lyric immediacy." To quote from Simic's introduction, they were poems of exploration "searching for an image" and "a flavor lost while he groped for its name . . . a light which he allowed to pass over his face without opening the eyes."[1] In these poems, the expanding universe becomes a metaphor for an eternal separation and estrangement, as in the mind-haunting conclusion to "The King and the Singer":

> And so in the end, your Excellency,
> we are powerless, both of us:
> From the wedding of this song
> comes a heaven, a more dangerous earth,
> and the multitudes we cannot control.
> And every night
> the familiar stars
> slip further and further away.

Bam! That poem has stayed with me for forty-one years, and as long as I have a memory, I will have it.

05/58 Gene Robards

The Metaphysical Giraffe, by Alvin Greenberg (New Rivers Press, 1968), cover and drawings by
Gene Robards.

reality, with mirrors

this is the stage
where we ought to
abolish paternal
illusions, this

the daughter who
comes on the stage
in tights, and this
the saw, the motto

of the aging father
in tails who has to
blink in the glare
though he does not

want to when that
band arrives with
horns, with tunes

and the curtain
awaits, and this
father who's there
while the audience

assembles and the
march begins peeks
through his fingers
at ticket sellers,

at ushers with red
hair, at multitudes
in the aisles, at

"reality, with mirrors," *The Metaphysical Giraffe*, by Alvin Greenberg (New Rivers Press, 1968),
cover and drawings by Gene Robards.

From those days I also remember Siv Cedering Fox's book of intelligently carnal lyrics, and Victor Contoski's beautiful meditations on immobility, and Contoski's own translations of contemporary Polish poetry. New Rivers had an international view in those days. And there were the political satires, too: a chapbook anthology titled *The Sensuous President by "K"*, for example, with poems by C. K. Williams and Robert Bly, among others.

In the early 1970s, the press was also a one-man band. How Bill managed it all, I'm not sure. I think that he believed that if he simply printed the books and sent out copies for review, the poetry world would beat a path to his office on West End Avenue. This misjudgment lasted during the years he was living in Manhattan, but he can't be blamed for it. The literary scene in New York often takes the form of social Darwinism, and I think Bill was shaken to discover how rigidly hierarchical it could be and how small presses would be scorned. New York's food chain was often shocking to him, and in any case he hated literary arbiters and poobahs and couldn't suck up to them even if he had wanted to. With this poobah-ism, it was difficult to counteract with reviews and phone calls, and Bill developed elaborate conspiracy theories having to do with who got what kind of attention.

To the best of my recollection of that time, the press did not advertise or engage in other forms of publicity. This absence was sometimes a sore point with New Rivers authors, but Bill did his best to get word out, writing to me in 1971 that he "was in Dallas last week doing the CCLM [Coordinating Council of Literary Magazines] trip and hating myself . . . and politicking and being loved as an editor stead of a poet . . . would do anything in the world to be fiddle again." He signed the letter: "Love, Borges."

Fiddle. Clyde. Borges. His "self" was complicated, a house of mirrors, a magnetic field whose shavings pointed inward. He had all these heteronyms, all these alternative personalities, and he liked to put them on display. Something about fixed identities seemed like a trap to him, and his poems from that period have the exhausted resignation of a long-time prisoner gazing through the bars of the cage. This is about New York City in the '70s:

> it is not so dark here
> as I expected
> in fact the streets are lively
> if violent
> there is laughter
> shocks of it and screams
> the streets shudder often
> you get used to that

Note the flat tonelessness. His poems tended to be private, often so private that you couldn't figure out what was being referred to or what was going on in them. The lines were blank, slack, nakedly despondent, and he seemed utterly bewildered by the world's indifference to them. In one letter to me, he denies being "bitter and despairing," but I think he often was. By contrast, his letters—he was a wonderful correspondent, as I've said—had a kind of manic playfulness, as did his political satires on the subject of Richard Nixon, and the playfulness erupted especially in the letters he sent from 205 West End Avenue and then in the poems from his book *Doctor Vertigo*, a collection that has his face on both the front and back cover and a funhouse mirror image of his face inside. One of his letters from 1970 begins: "doomsday was a kind of joyous liquid affair not at all what I expected and much warmer than December, and January's cruel vengeance is nowhere far behind— visions of mouths stuffed with words and APPLICATIONS. What was a veritable quest will be something else, though little."

Gradually he and I grew apart. I wouldn't say that we became estranged, but I often found myself on uncertain footing with Bill. One time, when I thought he was going through a bad period, I told him that I hoped he was all right, and he exploded in rage. What did I mean? What lay behind that remark? Another time, in Ann Arbor, we stopped at a gas station for a carton of cigarettes he needed, and I said, out of the blue, that maybe he should try to quit smoking. You didn't say things like that to Bill. Now that I am in my sixties, I know that you shouldn't offer advice to someone who hasn't asked for it, and you especially don't offer advice to an older man about habit-forming behaviors. But I was worried about him, so I did what you should not do, and after becoming furious at me, he sulked and would not speak to me for a long time afterward. Anyone who describes Bill Truesdale without mentioning his prickliness is not giving you the full portrait.

But I had a great deal to be grateful for, and I wanted him to know that, so when Paris Review Editions published a third book of my poems, *Imaginary Paintings*, many years later, I dedicated the book to him and sent him a copy. Silence. I waited. The calendar pages fell from the wall; the hands of the clock spun around and around. Finally, the next time I saw him, I asked him if he had received the book. He said he had. I mentioned that I had dedicated the book to him, and he thanked me. I asked him—I shouldn't have—if he had read it. *No*, he said, *he hadn't read it; he had been too busy*.

By that time, I wasn't really an underdog anymore, and he had lost interest in me because he could no longer help me out. It was the discoveries he loved, not the successes. Several of the poems in *The Loss of Rivers* are about fox hunting, and he did have some of the instincts of the hunter once he became an editor. By the late 1980s, I didn't require his aid and comfort, having had a few minor attainments, and for him the pleasure in the hunt was gone. Toward my good luck, such as it was, he directed the full force of his anger, which took the form of teasing and robust indifference. I'm not sure he realized what he was doing. One friend of his and mine has described with deadly accuracy an instance of Bill's teasing:

> He laughs when he announces he could easily pick me up and toss me out the window. He laughs to let me know he is just making a joke. But he *could* easily pick me up and toss me out the window. It is no joke. He also laughs to show me he knows it is no joke. And I laugh with him, of course, in order to let him know that I know that he knows it is no joke.

This is a fairly accurate description of the sort of interactions that Bill and I had after my fiction began to be published by commercial publishers in New York. It was as if I had engaged in a low form of betrayal. I had sold out. Whenever I saw him subsequently, he would find my weak spots, touch the wounds, and then worry them with teasing. The teasing was interminable, unbearable.

What I am trying to describe here is a human being in all his lovability and faults and contradictions. I loved him and then found myself avoiding him. In the 1960s and early 1970s, when I was shy, and tentative, and unrecognized, and needy, and vulnerable, and unknown, and hopeless, and desolate (the list of adjectives could go on for a long time), Bill Truesdale threw me one life preserver after another. He bucked me up and encouraged me and praised me and offered his hospitality time and again and filled me with confidence and hope. When I gained some confidence and had some recognition, he didn't know what to do with me, apart from the teasing, and he went his way, and I went mine.

In my life, I have known other human beings like Bill, who are generous as long as you need their generosity. This variety of patronage is an ideal mode for a small-press publisher, who is essentially throwing out life preservers to writers who may be in danger of drowning. When the books succeed, everybody wins: The culture benefits from the books and the writers' art, and the writers who thought that no attention would ever be paid to them discover that they *don't* have to die like dogs in the gutter or sink like stones in the pond. Something— some force, some benevolence—will hold them up, at least for a while.

We are sitting on the deck at Moccasin Lake. Bill is smoking a cigar, and Joan is reading Lawrence Ferlinghetti's *Her*. I have a new poem about which I am shyly proud, and I want to read it to them, and I am waiting for Bill or Joan to ask about it. Finally, Bill (let's say) asks to hear the poem. I am bursting with happiness. Also, I am a little drunk from the bourbon. Inside the cabin, the kids—Hardie and Stephanie and Anna—are playing a game, Monopoly, and chicken is roasting in the oven. From my pocket I pull out the poem, and, holding it up—my hands are shaking—I start to read it. Bill and Joan look intently at me while I intone it, a poem called "The Man with the Shovel." When I am finished, Joan smiles and nods, and Bill also nods his head, as if I had said something correct. "That's wonderful," he says. "It's scary and wonderful."

The year is 1969. People are suffering everywhere. But I could float away, such is my joy.

1. Ivan V. Lalić, *Fire Gardens* (New York: New Rivers Press, 1970), 10–11.

JOYCE SUTPHEN

This Beautiful Paper

Tonight, in an old notebook
on the reverse side of a scribbled

poem that never got off
the ground (a poem that kept

going back to the starting line
and flapping its paper wings),

I decided to be thankful for the pen
in a hand that can still hold it,

still make the ink into letters,
the letters into words that are

worlds no matter how tiny and
almost indecipherable. Tonight

I love the faint blue horizons
that cross the page, waiting

to be filled with golden light
as if in a Rembrandt painting.

Poet, teacher, and publisher, Mark Vinz is the author of more than fifteen poetry collections. His honors include three Minnesota Book Awards and, most recently, the Kay Sexton Award for fostering books, reading, and literary activity in Minnesota.

Remembering Bill Truesdale

"My life has become a complex series of dramatic encounters
with some of the most interesting persons in the world."
—C. W. Truesdale, in *The Talking of Hands*

As I was growing up, there were usually copies of *Reader's Digest Magazine* in our house. Beyond the various humorous vignettes in those pages, I always read the "The Most Unforgettable Character I Ever Met" essays. To this day, I can't see that title without thinking of C.W. "Bill" Truesdale. In so many ways he was both unforgettable and a character, but besides being a true eccentric, he was a remarkable visionary and pioneer in the world of small-press publishing for more than thirty years. He was also a good friend—one who prided himself on having had a great deal to do with the development of so many writers. And that certainly included me.

I can't remember when I met Bill for the first time, only that he was already a legendary figure and that I was prepared for a verbal assault that never came. In the late '70s, when New Rivers was based in New York, Bill began submitting books to the organization I was president of—Plains Distribution Service, a small-press distributor of work by midwestern writers and presses. Almost all the books Bill submitted for our quarterly booklists were rejected by our readers' committee, which, of course, greatly frustrated Bill and provoked questioning letters and phone calls. I'm happy to say that, eventually, some of the New Rivers books did get accepted, even before Bill had relocated in St. Paul and began focusing on the work of Midwestern writers. One thing is certain: With the move, the press began to change, especially with the start of the Minnesota Voices Project, an open competition in both poetry and prose for writers in the region, and the only one without an entry fee—something that Bill would continue to insist upon, no matter how much New Rivers needed the money.

In the second annual Minnesota Voices competition (1982), I entered a poetry manuscript, and even though my book was eventually rejected, I received an extremely detailed and encouraging rejection letter from Bill. Letters such as that one were something for which he became famous. I entered again the following year, this time with a prose poem manuscript, and ended up one of the four winners. My collection, *The Weird Kid*, was published later in 1983. Bill was one of the very few editors I had encountered who both appreciated and welcomed the prose poem form, which encouraged me to submit the manuscript in the first place. As he was to note later in his Publisher's Preface to the New Rivers prose poem anthology *The Party Train* (1996), Bill fervently believed the prose poem had been neglected by too many writers and largely ignored by literary critics, "despite the excitement the form has generated among poets themselves." As a writer, critic, editor, and publisher, he became a true champion of the prose poem.

Given the opportunity to work closely with Bill as a Minnesota Voices winner, I found his insights and suggestions invaluable, even if his sense of time and timing were not. Once the manuscript had been edited and we were in the process of going over the galleys, Bill phoned one day to ask how soon the artwork would be arriving in St. Paul. At this I panicked, for he'd never mentioned that he wanted me to find an artist for the book or that there was an honorarium for the job. Fortunately for us both, a friend at Moorhead State put me in touch with Anne Olson, a talented undergraduate art major. In very short order, this remarkable young woman produced a cover drawing and four interior plates for *The Weird Kid*, all of which handsomely illustrated various prose poems in the collection. Thanks to a daily courier service between Fargo-Moorhead and the Twin Cities, Bill was able to receive the drawings a matter of hours before the printer's deadline.

The Weird Kid, by Mark Vinz (New Rivers Press, 1983), cover design by Anne Olson, one of the first student art majors at Moorhead State University (now MSUM) to design a New Rivers Press cover.

One other image from those days remains etched in my memory—the one time I visited Bill at New Rivers Press in St. Paul. His office was crammed with stacks of papers and cardboard boxes. His desk might have appropriately been described as Dickensian; it was as if I'd seen it somewhere before, perhaps arising from the pages of *Bleak House*. Suddenly it became clear to me why Bill had never gotten around to informing me about the need for artwork: The letter he thought he'd sent was undoubtedly buried somewhere in one of those monumental piles on his desk.

Not long after the book was published, Bill asked me to serve as a Minnesota Voices Project judge, which I did for two years, reading boxes of manuscripts and sitting through some very long—but always cordially productive—meetings with Bill and my fellow judges. But we soon learned that Bill's vote occasionally seemed to be worth at least two of ours, for he was never shy about making detailed stands for his preferences. In spite of those always interesting times, two rounds of judging were enough to wear me out, though after Bill talked me into it, I eventually agreed to serve on the New Rivers board of directors. Little did I know that my term would last from 1988–1999, which I believe remains the longest tenure of any board member. Because of my own experience with small-press publishing, including my own Dacotah Territory Press, I felt a strong commitment to what Bill and New Rivers were accomplishing. It was also a way to keep up with what was going on in the region, and in contemporary literature in general, and I came to look forward to my quarterly trips to the Twin Cities for board meetings, even in times of turmoil and financial stress. We had some very difficult meetings, but Bill also had a knack for surrounding himself with workers who became more than employees—they were his loyal supporters and friends.

While Bill and I never had the chance to travel together during those years, we did attend some of the same literary events, such as small press book fairs. It's there that I find my favorite image of Bill, precariously lugging or wheeling boxes of books or simply sitting behind a table with his wares spread out in front of him, frequently wreathed in a cloud of cigarette smoke, and, of course, always telling stories with great animation. Bill was perhaps the only true raconteur I've ever known. His many fascinating experiences sometimes seemed like a series of separate lives; literary figures I could only dream of meeting, he knew intimately. Sometimes in my recollections, Bill's wife, Vivian, is there with him, too, and they're often bickering, though those who knew them also understood how truly devoted they were to each other. If at times Vivian seemed Bill's equal in chaotic disorganization, it was also clear they had found a way to keep each other going.

Several years after *The Weird Kid*, I completed a second collection of prose poems, which Bill agreed to read. In those days, the selection process was determined pretty much exclusively by Bill. I was delighted when he decided New Rivers should publish the collection, but rather than issue the new work as a separate volume, Bill wanted to combine it with *The Weird Kid*. With some trepidation, I agreed, and New Rivers published my "collected prose poems," *Late Night Calls,* in 1992. Though I eventually admitted that it was indeed a good idea to combine the work, I couldn't resist kidding Bill about the PhD he'd inadvertently given me in the book's bio note. He quickly responded by reminding me that even if he'd come to like me a great deal, he liked my wife, Betsy, even better.

It was about then that Robert Alexander joined the board (becoming a contributing editor and probably Bill's closest friend), and I came to eagerly anticipate the dinners with Robert and Bill after board meetings. At least in part because we got along well, and also because Robert had done his PhD dissertation on the prose poem, Robert proposed that the three of us edit what was to become *The Party Train: A Collection of North American Prose Poetry* (published by New Rivers in 1996), and Bill agreed. To say the least, we had some spirited debates as we were editing the manuscript (one that I lost was the selection of the title). But all in all, we were able to work very closely together on the project and I'm happy to say that all of our disagreements were resolved quite amicably.

Serving on the board in those years proved to be increasingly tumultuous, especially as New Rivers' financial difficulties increased. But I served with many thoughtful and dedicated board members and staff, and ultimately we weathered some very difficult storms. On the other hand, during this time I also edited Phil Bryant's MVP poetry collection, *Sermon on a Perfect Spring Day*, a project I truly enjoyed.

Since we had worked so well together on *The Party Train* (and had so much fun), Bill decided that he, Robert, and I should edit the New Rivers' thirtieth anniversary volume, published in 1998 as *The Talking of Hands* (another title I voted against but lost). As we had done in the editing of *The Party Train*, two of us would pick work by the third, though Bill eventually decided that his short history of New Rivers would stand as his entry. It came as no surprise that he insisted I submit some recently written prose poems.

When the book was published, we had a grand celebration and reading at the Landmark Center in St. Paul. Close to one hundred New Rivers authors had submitted manuscripts for the anthology, though we were only able to accept work by about half of those authors; I remember all too well making several well-discussed and painful rejections. As for what the book should encompass, we decided to ask for previously unpublished work as opposed to putting together a retrospective anthology. Emphasizing the *new* in the press's title, the anthology looked forward rather than back, which fit both Bill's personality and his continuing vision for the press. It was also a great pleasure to read those submissions, many from authors Bill had literally discovered, and many of whom I had not previously read. As David Haynes wrote of the press's publishing record in his introduction to the volume, "How many of those books might never have seen print were it not for the courage of New Rivers to take a chance on the unknown writer and the unfashionable idea."

The celebration of New Rivers' anniversary was darkened by Bill's deteriorating health. All of us who worked with him knew that his days as head of New Rivers were numbered. He was madly writing his memoir (parts of which he sent to several of us for corrections or updates), and while distance makes my memory of the final days of New Rivers in Minneapolis a bit blurry, I vividly remember visiting Bill in a nursing home in a Twin Cities suburb a couple of months before he died. Although his congestive heart failure had really taken its toll, he was the same old Bill in spirit—full of stories and excited about writing his memoir. As I left, he winked and reminded me one last time that as much as he liked me, he liked Betsy better.

In so many different ways over the years, Bill provided an invaluable education for me as a writer, an editor, and a teacher. And, as many have pointed out, New Rivers was responsible for publishing an amazing variety and quantity of imaginative writing—poetry, fiction, and nonfiction—and perhaps even more importantly, for providing encouragement and support for a large number of writers. As he wrote in "New Rivers Press: A History (1968-1998)," which was published first in *The Talking of Hands*, "[his] own interest lay in the book itself and what it had to say or what it actually created." That's indeed the way the press was founded and maintained—not on politics or movements, and certainly not on self-aggrandizement. In the same essay, Bill continued:

> It is important for me to earn the respect of the authors I deal so often with, to establish a confidence in them that I can be of help or service to them, and that I can bring a good deal of experience and critical intelligence to this work.

And so he did, unforgettably.

Deborah Keenan

HOUSEHOLD WOUNDS

Household Wounds, by Deborah Keenan (New Rivers Press, 1981), prizewinner of the very first Minnesota Voices Project (now Many Voices Project).

DEBORAH KEENAN

Deborah Keenan, former editor for Milkweed Editions, now teaches creative writing at Hamline University. She is the recipient of multiple awards, including in 1991, the American Book Award. She was New Rivers Press's first winner of the Minnesota Voices Project (now the Many Voices Project) prize for poetry.

New Rivers, Bill Truesdale, Years Go By: How Memory Works

I first knew *of* Bill Truesdale. Then I knew him. I was part of the Macalester College community at that time. My first husband, Michael Keenan, was part of the English faculty, and because of my slightly odd balancing act as student and faculty wife, I found my first writing community in my close friendships with Wendy Parrish and Al Greenberg. Both had placed books with New Rivers, and it was certainly the first and deepest introduction I had to the world of independent presses, since I read and loved their books. Bill Truesdale was part of, and apart from the social community, but he did let me know of his new publishing venture called Minnesota Voices, and I decided to submit the book I had been working on throughout my twenties, called *Household Wounds*. I had been writing furiously and seriously for several years, and I remember well my beloved typewriter, and the many drafts of each poem, and how I dreaded submitting work with any typographical errors, and though I had seen errors in some New Rivers books I wanted my submission to be as strong as I could make it. So I sent the manuscript to New Rivers, continued sending poems out to magazines, and waited.

Bill called to tell me the judges had selected my manuscript and I still remember that phone call: my surprise and joy, and his happiness for me. He told me he had read the book carefully, and wanted to meet to discuss the poems. It was the late '70s, I was newly divorced with two little kids, and I was just beginning to make my way into the larger writing community. His office, on Selby Avenue in St. Paul, was pretty much a book addict's delight; it was jammed with books against every wall, and piled high on the tables and floor, it was also full of the smell of books and cigarette smoke, and when I walked in I remember thinking that this was the real world of publishing. I laugh now, when I think of the beautiful offices of the independent presses in the Twin Cities, but then it was a kind of paradise to me. I cleared a chair and sat down, and Bill told me immediately that the four villanelles and sestinas that I had included in the manuscript had to go, that I was a free verse poet, and these received forms did not suit the spirit of my book. I nodded and offered no argument. I had used one curse word in one poem, and he told me it had to go—that the voice in my book was not a voice that swore. I nodded. Finally he told me that my book was wonderful, but so sad. Poems about Vietnam, about my friend Wendy's death, my father's suicide, were all fine poems, but he wanted me to go home and create a poem that could conclude the book with a bit of hope. I said I would, and we scheduled our next meeting and I left, dazed, wondering about what hopeful poem I might be able to conjure.

Two weeks later I returned with a new final poem, which he approved. We went over the structure of the book and the table of contents, and he asked what color I wanted for my cover. He fanned out cards of colors; I chose a deep red. He asked if I wanted illustrations. At that time I was working with Gaylord Schanilec, now a famous artist and letterpress printer, but at that time we worked together at COMPAS, a community arts organization, and he was busy creating a letterpress book of a small set of angel poems I had written. His press, Midnight Paper Sales Press—named in honor of the paper discarded into trash bins outside paper companies which he then used for his press—was in downtown St. Paul, and I would run over there after work to stare at my words being typeset, and at the images of angels he created and was printing for that limited edition book, *One Angel Then*. I told Bill I would love to have Gaylord draw something for the cover, and he said that was fine with him. Gaylord created a beautiful ink drawing of a piece of fabric with a needle moving through it for the cover, and then for each section, the same fabric, with the needle moving to a new place in the fabric. Bill told me to find a black and white photograph of myself, and to get that—and a two-sentence bio statement—to him. He told me he had chosen black end papers, which he felt went well with the red cover.

I remember being slightly intimidated by Bill—he was a big man, and his opinions were presented forcefully. I also remember feeling fortunate that I was inside this process, which I had dreamed of, and that he seemed to believe in my work, and in this new publishing venture he was adding to his extraordinary mix of American writers, and international writers. (Right before my book came out, Bill said he liked Gaylord's drawing and his laconic, steady way of being in the world, and asked him to illustrate the book *Unease*, by the great

Polish writer, Tadeusz Rozewicz. The woodcuts Gaylord created are extraordinary, and the translations by Victor Contoski brought Rozewicz into my consciousness and keep him there, still. I remember the thrill when Bill offered me a copy of this book; I still have it and I teach from it.)

At one of our meetings on Selby Avenue, Bill explained that he wanted no back-of-book statements from other writers for *Household Wounds*. He told me he thought they added nothing to a book and were just a way of playing politics in the literary world. He also told me the book would retail for three dollars, that he believed in a world where all books could be owned by any person, whatever their income was.

I always tell my students to celebrate when their first book comes out, and to remember the feeling. For me, *Household Wounds* becoming a book in the real, material world, was thrilling. New Rivers Press opened the door at the beginning of my career as a published writer, and it has been easy for me to reconnect with that sense of excitement and gratitude over the many years since its publication. Bill was pleased for me, in his gruff way. I think he liked being in at the start of people's careers, and I believe he took real pleasure in watching his Minnesota Voices series grow each year. These were the olden days, where funding for a press was perhaps a bit easier to secure—the books sold well, and each year a different set of judges would choose one and then two books for the new series. Many writing careers were launched through New Rivers, and I remember being at all kinds of publication events those early years, celebrating the writers whose books were selected after *Household Wounds*.

Bill attended only one of my publication readings. I don't have a sense that readings given by other writers gave him that much joy; I could be wrong. It was the start of that time in American publishing where writers presented their books to the public in this way—a time when independent, not-for-profit presses were starting to understand that they had to have marketing plans and venues for their writers to read in, and it was a real move away from the times when a book would come into the culture and somehow that book might be found by a reader. At the reading of mine that Bill attended, all I really remember is Bill taking my hands and saying, "Someone is going to have to cut off these hands." Of course I was shocked, but he went on to say that I was too expressive with my hands when I read, which was distracting for the audience. I listened, but it did give me a chill, and I do remember that moment all these years later.

Household Wounds sold well, and I would occasionally see Bill at parties or visit him at his office or at O'Garas, a bar and restaurant at the corner of Selby and Snelling, just a few steps from his office, where he conducted more and more of his press business. At that time, and I may be remembering this incorrectly, Bill rarely published authors a second time who were part of the Minnesota Voices series. He said his job was to launch new voices, and so I was surprised a few years later when he asked if I had another manuscript ready to go. I did. I sent him my fourth book, *The Only Window That Counts*, and he called to say he liked it, that he wanted to publish it, and had no editorial suggestions for me. The week of his call I had been working on a long poem, "Greenland Mummy," and I felt it needed to be in the manuscript. I told him I had a new poem I thought was right for the manuscript, and he asked me to meet him at O'Garas. He read the poem and agreed it fit the spirit of the new book, but he was concerned the book would be too long if we included it. I told him I would trade three other poems in the book if "Greenland Mummy" could be included. He laughed, asked me what three poems, and as I tried to figure out what to pull from the manuscript he smiled and said not to worry about it, that the new poem would be the right ending for this new book, and he would keep the manuscript as it was.

We had only one more meeting about the book. Again, I was offered my choice of artist to work with, and I brought in Tim Francisco's wonderful photographs. We selected one for the cover, and four more to use as visual moments in the book, which was structured in sections. Tim also took the author photo, and once again Bill chose black endpapers, and insisted on no statements from other writers for the back cover. It is hard to explain how simple the process seemed to me. I was still a young writer, and I had total trust in Bill's way of perceiving the world of publishing.

The Only Window That Counts was published, sold well, and went into a second printing. Bill was not present at any of the readings. At that time, the magazine *Minnesota Monthly* published lots of writing by local and regional writers. The editors there selected several poems from this book to print, and I know that helped me make my way as a writer in my community.

Bill and I stayed in touch, notes and calls a few times a year. We were not friends, I guess, though perhaps we were. He was, for me, a difficult person to figure out, and sometimes difficult to figure out how to interact with. We were most comfortable when talking about books, smoking in his small office or meeting at O'Garas. We fit in our roles then, I guess: a new writer, and a publisher who seemed to me to know how to operate in the publishing world. My sense of gratitude for Bill Truesdale's power and influence in my writing career has never diminished. I think the last time I saw him I had accepted an invitation to his home for a picnic. He seemed not particularly healthy to me that afternoon. I remember worrying about how he was doing, but we certainly did not talk about it. I drove home in a blinding thunderstorm, one of those storms where you cannot see, and you pray that you can pull to the side of the freeway safely, not be slammed from behind by another car, another driver blinded by rain and lightning. I sat in my car at the side of the freeway for at least half an hour. Bill had given me a couple of recently published New Rivers books when we had said goodbye, and I sat in my car reading them while waiting for the rain to stop. I remember that once I was safely off the freeway I was happy to be sitting in my old car, reading.

My bookshelves still hold many New Rivers books. Students of mine, friends of mine, are part of the long history of New Rivers books, and I certainly feel a sense of community with many of them. As I said before, I feel fortunate to be a New Rivers Press author, and I feel I owe a great debt of gratitude to Bill Truesdale for helping me make my way as a poet in America.

DAVID HAYNES

David Haynes is the author of six critically acclaimed novels—three of them published by New Rivers Press—and five children's books. A former board member for New Rivers Press, he is now the director of creative writing at Southern Methodist University in Dallas, TX.

The Greater Good

Tony, one of my Facebook buds, updates the condition of the powder at Telluride, and he makes it every bit as alluring as he did the coral reefs of Bora Bora, where he honeymooned last spring. Tony is a former student, an alumnus of my employer, a genuine one-percenter, as have been many of my charges here in Dallas. I confess that now and again I experience a twinge of envy over his reports from the world of the rich and excessive. Similar in its prickliness to the flush of resentment I feel when watching house porn on HGTV, rather than admit that there might be some pleasure inside that 800-square-foot kitchen—the one with the warming drawers and the six-burner gas range—I instead prefer to imagine that the white marble floors become stained with cranberry juice and the cabinet fronts quite quickly becoming as outdated and as tired as the cheap laminate has in my own home. As for Telluride, mountains give me vertigo, and I prefer not to go outside when the temperature is below 45 degrees.

Like many working-class people, I grew up in a family who believed that stuff confers status, partially a logical consequence of not having any to begin with, but also largely the result of being steeped, as we all are, in the messages of a consumer culture, where the more the better and the better the best. That these messages never stuck is one of the many minor miracles of my life. Prada? Armani? I have almost no idea what those things actually mean. I wear the same shoes every day and, as I am writing this, the clothes on my back cost a total of maybe thirty bucks, depending on how you aggregate the multipack of socks and briefs from the discount store. I have owned the T-shirt I am wearing since sometime in the Clinton administration.

Growing up, we had this next-door neighbor, Mildred White, who took an interest in me, hauling me away on regular excursions to the library and the art museum. Once, when I was a young teen, she baited me with a question about my career aspirations. I told her I was committed to doing something "interesting" with my life. She scoffed. Did I imagine, she wondered, that my father enjoyed going off to the auto body shop every day? People did jobs to make money, she admonished me, and I was also advised to get the hell over myself, or whatever the late '60s equivalent of that might have been. I am pleased to report this as another example of guidance from the adult world that failed to take root.

In college, friends (LOTS of them) baffled me with their admissions of little or no interest in their chosen careers. But a person had to do something, after all, so why not make a lot of money at a law firm. Fleetingly, I, too, would entertain the notion of pursuing majors that promised to lead to a future full of riches and contentment, but ciphering bores me (as do lawyers), and thus my college years were full of lamentations from the family over my lack of interest in the sorts of jobs that might lead to "the good life." Surely I would come to my senses, and I know that they counted on the ravages of hunger and the charms of low income housing to facilitate sensible decision-making on my part.

For better or worse, I chose this life on the margins. I have managed to avoid living in any place genuinely awful and have maintained more than a healthy weight. I entertained few illusions about getting rich pursuing the life of a teacher and a writer. (Which isn't to say that the publication of each of my novels didn't also coincide with a few shiny fantasies of best-seller lists and a seat in the comfy butter-yellow leather chair next to Oprah, but among my marketable traits is that I am a realist who also happens to come from a family of stoics.) My borderline career, while occasionally annoying, has never caused me much stress. Like infected hangnails, career angst tends to resolve over time into the general ache that is known as being alive. And if it doesn't, you bite it off at the quick and keep moving forward. Scarlett was right: Tomorrow *is* another day.

But, then, I have been slightly disingenuous about my lack of jealousy for the one percent: It's not their money that I envy; it's the not having to think about money that makes me want to start the revolution now. In the marginal world of the arts and of public education, the locale of my early professional life, we think about money all the time, or, more specifically, we think about the lack of it. In the world of the small press, the wolf is always at the door, and even in the rare season—when a book sells well or when the funders are extra generous—like children of the Great Depression, you hoard the dregs of the flour barrel, add an extra can of water to that pot of soup, and keep working that bar of soap until its last sliver dissolves in your fingers. Hard times will return. They always do.

But it's what we signed up for, after all. What's the use complaining?

***

I do not go to parties. They make me uncomfortable.

But my friend Sanderia does, and since she'd been riding shotgun throughout the conference I agreed to board the specially designated elevators to the penthouse for the evening's festivities. Earlier in the year I'd been elected to the Association of Writers and Publishers board of directors, thus the invitation to the VIP reception.

It was a fancy joint, let me tell you: restored late Gilded Age glamour, all gold sconces and velvet-flocked wallpapers. The dark void through the French doors was Lake Michigan, a mighty spectacular view, one imagined, on a warm summer day. This was March, close to midnight and well below freezing outside. I didn't care to step out onto the balcony to take in the icy shores, but plenty of others did. Writers. They can never resist a scenic overlook.

Sanderia and I loaded up a plate of really mediocre hors d'oeuvres (one would expect a big, name-brand Michigan Avenue hotel to do more than cube up some generic cheese; one would be wrong) and settled ourselves in on one of the few couches in the room—because, seriously, if I was going to be uncomfortable, at least I was going to be comfortable. We set about my favorite hobby: checking out all the people in the room and making up lies about them.

Many of our fellow partygoers were seriously famous, inasmuch as there is such a thing as literary fame—which as best as I can tell means being famous mostly only to the other people in the parlor—and some of the lies that we invented from our couch were nothing less than spectacular. (I particularly liked the one about the former poetry ingénue, now well past her sell-by date, but still working hard her persona as the mild-mannered milkmaid of the prairie.) I'm wagering half of our speculations were relatively close to accurate: We know how writers operate, after all, and like all good storytellers, it works well to base one's falsehoods close to the truth. It keeps the court costs to a minimum.

Mentor/muse Carol Bly once claimed that this literary world we occupy is zero degrees of separation small. In fairness, her perceptions of the size of things may have been shaped by the way that for decades the major players in that world made the pilgrimage to visit her and her ex on the farm out in western Minnesota, where the kitchen table was also the home of the legendary small presses of the '50s, '60s, and '70s. But even those of us much further removed from the white-hot center of the literary universe find our circles overlapping as richly as the most rococo Venn diagram. Just the other day I discovered I had been in the home of one of my students in the MFA Program for Writers at Warren Wilson. I know her husband but had never met her. They have different last names. Despite the intensity of all of the storming and steaming, we simmer in a small teapot, and if you stay in the game, your bubble eventually bumps up against most of the others. My dubious physics aside, I did know many of people in that penthouse, by name or by reputation.

As I'm sure you know, people have a lot of nerve and at one point, a group of party guests gathered for a photo next to the fireplace, conveniently and appropriately located at the end of my couch. For the record, my personal space requirements can be daunting. (Anywhere within fifty feet might be considered a violation: Consider yourself warned.) So, hell, yes, I got annoyed at all that smiling and posing and snapping. Who expects this level of mirth at a work function?

A week or so later, back home in Dallas, browsing the world's great equalizer—Facebook—I came across that set of photos and I realized that I'd been in correspondence with two of those smilers, within the month—one to judge Southern Methodist University's undergraduate poetry prize, the other to be a reader at our annual literary festival. I am glad that I did not suggest they back the hell away.

A bit later, back in the penthouse, the smilers were replaced by another group of jolly revelers. I rolled my eyes and Sanderia told me to behave. Like everyone else at the party, this crew seemed vaguely familiar, the way people you sit across the aisle from on the plane and later share a shuttle to the hotel seem familiar. One nods in a neutral sort of way and continues about one's business. Everyone at the damn party seemed similarly familiar. Like mayonnaise, writers come in a limited variety of flavors. These usurpers lingered, so I looked closer.

Skipping through the "and then I realized" false epiphany, I soon found myself in conversation with a fine cross selection of the old crew from New Rivers Press: Alan, Thom, and Robert. A few decades earlier, in various configurations, we'd sat around tables at the offices in Minneapolis, discussing book projects or planning the future of the press. Many of those are happy memories, others less so, and some will no doubt be recounted elsewhere as the anniversary of this important institution is celebrated. That it survived—that any small press survives and thrives—is as remarkable as is the fact that so many in the New Rivers family found themselves gathered by MY couch in a hotel penthouse in

Chicago. Who better to be toasted high above Michigan Avenue than publishers, editors, and writers who, on a pocketful of cash that has been begged, borrowed, or otherwise procured, keep the literary fire burning.

***

With rare exceptions, my teaching and artistic career has been affiliated with institutions that might generously be described as marginal. On the teaching side, this was quite intentional, as I made the choice to work in schools where I thought my services were most needed, where I thought I would make the most difference.

On the art side: Well, let's make a list of not-for-profit arts organizations that aren't marginal, shall we? And then let's remind ourselves that even the big museums make do with volunteer docents and are selling parts of their collections to keep the doors open all the while major symphonies, operas, and dance companies are closing theirs. And in any case, my own artistic endeavors intersected only rarely with that part of the stratosphere, and when it did I'd have to borrow a tie before shambling into the event. In every aspect of my life it has been the shoestring operations where I was most comfortable or most welcome or both. For what it's worth, I understand what it's like to be forced to make do with what you have.

I spent part of one summer at an art colony where some guy who stopped in to visit a friend was appointed "acting director." Now and again, he and the woman who had been sharing a ride with him to California before he got waylaid and appointed to his first position as an arts administrator would emerge from their love nest in the woods to check in on the colonists to see if we were still alive and thriving, and, no, he didn't happen to know where they kept the bear repellant or if his board of directors (whom he'd yet to meet in person) intended to restock the pantry.

I worked in an elementary school where our intrepid faculty assistant, Caroline, had invented various magical ways of reusing mimeograph paper for up to as many as a dozen passes through the spirit master machine. Each sodden math worksheet retained for hours the alluring aroma of industrial solvents, and, sadly, we no doubt contributed to a generation of inhalant abusers across the Twin Cities.

During my years at that school, I kept a giant coffee can full of broken crayons at the ready for art projects. In our little world, fresh unbroken colors were cherished like diamonds; you locked them up with the petty cash and an equally valuable commodity, the official hall pass. A busted up crayon with enough length to grasp in the fingers was a rare treat. And—bonus—if you kept the coffee can parked on the radiator, they'd melt together a bit, allowing the kids to create unexpected two- or three-striped effects on the page. Such a brilliant invention this is, you can now buy it directly from the Crayola mother ship, but speaking from my own experience as an underserved youth, I'm saddened to report that the charms of serendipitous art discoveries are lost on children whose life's dreams include their own virgin box of sixty-four unbroken colors. We made do, but we all felt a little bit cheated.

Many years, we rationed writing paper: a highlight of the teaching day, the shared shame of grudgingly sliding one precious sheet across the desk to a child chagrined by the need to ask for it. Our home-school liaison and secretary kept a stash of coats and gloves and hats in the backroom. I hoarded bags of apples and cookies in my supply closet: We had a late lunch and many of the kids couldn't afford to bring a snack.

I could go on and on and on, but I would hope you have been paying attention to life on the margins in America and would, therefore, find my recap redundant. There's something trashy about stories like this, isn't there? For too many people, suffering narratives become a kind of fetish: We get a rush from reports of pain, find virtue in our noble attentions to the worlds of the less fortunate, and perhaps a bit of relief from our own suffering when we open up the checkbooks to help out a bit.

But I am being snarkier than I wish to: Attention is important and good. Attentive people do open up their wallets, and thank God for that. Now and again a case of drawing paper appears unbidden on the loading dock of your neighborhood school; someone underwrites the bus for the field trip to the Minnesota Zoo.

It is also far too easy to create false equivalences between the issues connected to material poverty and those connected to cultural poverty.

Sandwiches versus books: Discuss.

My former colleague, Barbra Smith, used to insist, feed the kids first, and there's no arguing with that. Having stakes in several of these games, having benefited from as well as been the distributor of reduced lunch tickets to students in schools that also had solid arts programming, having seen the enduring impact that a visiting poet can have on a young life by paying a bit of attention to a disenfranchised young writer's words, I am perhaps too close to the case to argue one way or another.

Let's just say, then, that we in the arts and education communities are grateful for the wisdom of philanthropists, foundations, and funders whose answer to the bread versus books question is an enthusiastic, "Yes. Both."

***

An advantage to spending the weekend and summer vacations hanging around my father's auto body shop was that I found nothing particularly disturbing about the old New Rivers offices in Minneapolis. Disturbing, in the sense that a person with more delicate aesthetic sensibilities would have been inclined to open the door to Bill Truesdale's aerie in the Ford Building and say, "Yikes! How the hell is a book or anything the hell else going to be produced out of this dump?"

Or, perhaps it was that I had spent plenty of time in my Macalester mentor Arnie Holtz's lair in the basement of the ancient Carnegie building, which shared with the New Rivers offices the sense that a long series of manuscript lovers had inhabited this cave since the invention of paper. A person's absolute confidence that old Arnie or Bill could reach into those piles of chaos and hand you any specific piece of paper you requested battled with an equally strong sense that someone had set a bomb off in the file cabinet and that all of this shit remained exactly where it had landed after the explosion; that this had almost certainly happened decades earlier, thereby explaining the dust settled on the various random stacks.

About two decades after my first visit to the Ford Building, I attended a board meeting in a borrowed space in the high-rise offices of one of the major publishers in Manhattan. It hadn't occurred to me at the time that this monolith also housed a subsidiary of a subsidiary that had published my own most recent novel. There would be nothing in the environment to remind me or anyone else of this fact, so far down the pecking order was that particular subsidiary and, therefore, my humble little novel, within the hierarchy. Stunning displays in the marble and steel lobby touted the latest titles from the conglomerate, titles also assured equally prominent face time to the passersby in the windows of major retailers across the city and the world.

The board met in a conference room, and out the window behind the president of the organization, a rank of skyscrapers framed a vista of Central Park, all crimson and gold in its autumnal splendor. As was the lobby, the conference room had been lined with the leading products of this particular manufacturer, faced out on oak shelving, titles by writers we all have heard of. A few of those writers I knew personally, and this time I admit my jealousy right upfront.

But as before, this is envy of the askew variety: not that these books were with a major publisher, while mine were not; as mentioned before, like Oedipus, I had, in fact, already dated these particular family members.

Instead, it was the preciousness of it all that made me sad for the less glorified fate of my own neglected children. All that expertly joined woodwork, the elegant gallery lighting, with each spot carefully aimed at each individual book jacket. This whole office building as much as a temple to the printed word. I rocked gently in my leather upholstered chair and took it all in. No one had had to clear a pile of manuscripts from that chair so I could make myself comfortable.

To be clear, by "no one," I mean Bill. Not that Bill was no one—far from it—but rather to say that there was no tower full of minions around to sort and organize and decorate the offices at the Ford Building. For *many* years it was just Bill in that office, supplemented by a Katie or a Michelle or a Jim or various other brilliant young interns, sacrificing a few years of their lives for the greater good. Sometimes there was grant money to retain them for a year or two beyond their internships, to offer them a title and a bit of money for their hard work. Sometimes there was not, and sometimes there simply wasn't anybody else there at all other than Bill.

And there it is, another story of life on the margins, small arts organization edition. Anyone with passing interest in the literary world can recite the details of many similar enterprises. Invited to dinner, we sip wine around the dining room table as editor and spouse file away and box the contents of the September issue in order to make way for the carrot loaf. We've ridden shotgun with the graduate assistant tasked to search the campus loading docks for the shipment from the printer.

And once again I wander toward that dicey boundary where life on the margins can begin to seem glamorous in the shabby chic way of the hole-in-the-wall greasy spoon with the great blueberry pancakes. The foodies line up, oblivious to the fact that they pay the employees crap, miffed all the same at the egg residue on the tines of each and every fork.

The offices of New Rivers Press have never been glamorous, any more than was my father's auto body shop. Neither was there anything the least bit shameful about either place of business. They were humble places of work that well served the functional needs of their founders and owners. My job at the auto body shop was to sweep away the dust created by grinding away at the Bondo-covered fenders, to spread and scoop up the sawdust used to soak up the oil and grease that leaked from engines. (They knew better than to trust me with the acetylene torches.) What might have seemed dirty and disorganized was in reality a fully functional workplace that provided well if modestly for our family. The only ornamentation was the vulgar pinup calendars given out each December by the auto salvage yards. Who needed decorations: This was a place of work, and God help you if you got too zealous with your cleaning. Leave my damn coffee cup right where I always leave it, damn you, and straighten those papers or move that box of wrenches and you are likely to lose a limb.

Cars emerged from those garage doors as shiny and new as the day they left the factory, and NRP books stand proudly on the shelves next to titles from the towers of New York. And unlike at those towers,

I was always confident someone among the pile of clutter knew my name, just as my father knew each and every one of his customers. There was always time for a chat with the folks at New Rivers Press.

***

Or for a conversation in the Penthouse of a fancy hotel on the lakefront in Chicago.

What a happy reunion that was. We did not discuss it that night, but we all knew the story of New Rivers could have been very different, that it was more likely the press would be only a historical memory than that it lives on and continues to do fine work.

That there does remain a New Rivers Press is a testament to the dedication, hard work, and deep belief of many people in the importance of this press in particular and of small presses in general. Bad things are happening in those towers in New York. This is not a secret. Whatever it is that goes on up there, little of it has much to do with poetry or serious literary fiction or in the belief in the importance of books and literature to our culture.

If serious writing is to survive in this country, it will be because New Rivers and its sister small presses survive and flourish. I intend to do what I can to make sure that is the case.

This is where I skip the part of the story where high above Michigan Avenue, I sheepishly but shamelessly pitched my current manuscript to Alan, which means I also skip the part where Sanderia stood behind me with a taser, daring me to lose my nerve.

It's good to have pushy friends.

In fact, I had intended to send *A Star in the Face of the Sky* to New Rivers for several years, but a number of roadblocks delayed me from doing so. I couldn't be more thrilled to be working with the press that started my career, and I am equally excited to work with the press to help invent the future of publishing.

Together, we will learn how smaller presses can collaborate with mid-list authors to sustain and extend careers.

We will discover together how to use social media and the Internet to find audiences for our books.

We'll figure out the way that actual books and e-books can co-exist in the marketplace.

We will make a bit of money perhaps, and we'll have a lot of fun doing it. It's going to be an interesting journey.

***

Likely neither Bill Truesdale nor my father would know what to make of some of the ways the world has changed since they left us. My father gave up his shop about the time that the computers in the engines began to make it impossible for him to tinker to a fix. That he was in his eighties at the time is another matter, but he would have worked there to his last breath, I've no doubt, if my brother hadn't taken over from him and those damn computers hadn't been so confounding. (For the record, he also absolutely refused to learn how an ATM worked and never watched one thing on a television set that was not broadcast through the air, the old-fashioned way, the way he liked it.)

Bill, too, went out with his boots on. (Which was kind of a problem for the press, but that'll have to be the subject of someone else's essay.) I can imagine him rolling his eyes at the screen on my Kindle. Bill enjoyed the feel of paper. He used to set books by hand, was familiar with ink under the fingernails. I am imagining he and my daddy comparing hands. I wonder if Bill used Goop to clean his?

But there I go again, romanticizing life on the margins, and the main problem with that is that those men didn't for one minute see their work as in any way marginal. Or romantic. It's what they did. It was their life.

***

In addition to Tony's missives from luxury resorts, my Facebook feed is also full of reports from the higher echelon of the publishing world. In place of powdery beaches and pristine slopes, here are the dazzling accounts of six-figure, two-book deals, multi-city book tours, and publication parties with people who are more important than you are. These posts tell a lie about the reality of the literary world in the same way that house porn and celebrity journalism misrepresent how the real world actually works.

But it's my own prickliness, I guess, at the reports of excess that directs my attention away from all those other wonderful posts I receive, documenting our vibrant contemporary literary life. Exciting news about new quarterlies and revived presses and innovative reading series. I curate a blog that documents the achievements of the students and faculty of an MFA program, and it's heartening to see all of that work being published, in print and online, and to have even a small part in helping it find an audience.

None of us are getting rich and none of us are ashamed about that either.

The following letter, written by C.W. "Bill" Truesdale and addressed to the members of the board of directors, reflects a major transitional period for the press as Truesdale officially relinquishes his position as Publisher.

The Future Status of New Rivers Press (November 20, 1998)

*T*o the New Rivers Board of Directors:

The questions of whether New Rivers Press is essentially a "founder-driven organization" and of what will happen to it when the founder is no longer connected with it has been discussed by the Board of Directors and has been raised by some consultants and funding organizations as well. One or two of these organizations have suggested that we simply close down.

This is something that I, as founder of New Rivers, have given a lot of thought to in recent years and one upon which I have very strong opinions. I know as well as anyone that I will reach my 70th birthday in March 1999, somewhat past the normal age of retirement (65 years). It is obvious to me that 1) I am reaching the age where my continued service to the organization will either cease altogether or gradually diminish; 2) at the present time I have no desire to "retire" but have worked out a diminishing service arrangement with the Board. On April 1, 1999, I will step down as "Publisher" and become "Senior Editor." As far as I am concerned, that change in status has already been taking place with the gradual restriction of my activities to the editorial side of the operation.

The big question facing the Board is not so much the vision of what New Rivers is all about, but whether the stimulation of new writing in this region and elsewhere is wholly dependent on me; and whether the press should continue. That vision has been somewhat modified over the years to reflect the essentially regional publication of books by individual writers (though a great many of them, including the Minnesota Voices Project winners, were not born and raised in this area). What began as basically a poetry press now includes short stories, novellas, familiar essays, and memoirs as well. I still consider New Rivers a "national" or even an "international" operation even though most of the books we publish by individual writers have originated in this area.

There are several things that need to be said in response to the original statement that New Rivers is "a founder-driven organization" and should close when I am no longer around as publisher:

1) Although I have certainly been personally involved in the operation of New Rivers and in its mission or vision from its very small beginnings back in 1968, I do not consider it "a founder-driven organization." I am a writer first and foremost. I have always seen publishing as an extension of that activity and not *vice versa*. Even when I did almost everything connected with the press by myself (which has not been the case for more than fifteen years now), I always regularly consulted others and have never sought to publish poets and writers who are "clones" of myself. Perhaps because of my academic background and my love for the great heritage of English, American, and world literature, I am aware of the tremendous diversity in first-rate literary expression and it has always been my intention to honor that diversity. I probably know as much as just about anyone about small press publications in this country and (to a lesser extent) abroad. I still read widely in a large variety of fields and disciplines and have written about a great many different subjects. And, since I can't possibly edit everything we publish, I generally look for editors who are similarly grounded as to background, but who are also independent of mind and judgment. In this respect, New Rivers has always had the reputation for being eclectic in its range of publications but focused on the quality of the writing we publish.

2) About fifteen years ago, I began to realize that I simply could not do all that was connected with the press and still continue writing. At that time, I was doing just about everything (except for the typesetting and distribution)—fund-raising, layout, correspondence, order filling, manuscript reading, accounting, and so forth. The Board of Directors, particularly one Board member—the late Roger Blakely, a professor at Macalester College—was very supportive of me. Roger saw to it that I had regular part-time help from various Macalester students—Daren Sinsheimer first, then Linda Ascher, and finally Katie Maehr. Blakely, Jonis Agee (another writer and Board member), John Minczeski (a New Rivers author), Vivian Balfour (who eventually became my wife and a Board member), Mark Vinz, Robert Alexander (both New Rivers authors and Board members), and others took on some of the editorial work. When Katie graduated from

Macalester, she became our first full-time employee. Though very young at the time, she quickly began to demonstrate an amazing capability in every aspect of our interestingly complex organization and became our first Managing Editor. Katie took on more and more of the day-to-day work of the press, a delegation of authority and responsibility that I willingly surrendered. When she left the organization after five rich years, she went on to graduate school with my blessing, though I was very reluctant to lose her.

The real point of my recounting this story now is that I began to realize that I was eventually going to have to step down and that New Rivers would continue to flourish long after I was no longer part of the organization. Maehr—perhaps inadvertently—was teaching me that no one person was indispensable to an organization and that what I originally envisioned as the primary mission of New Rivers could be carried on by someone else. If not Katie, then certainly another individual.

3) Once the Minnesota Voices Project was established in 1981, I immediately saw it as essential that the winning manuscripts ought to be selected by a panel of first three, then five judges—always including me as Publisher and Chief Editor of New Rivers. It is true that the other panelists were always selected by me but I saw it as very important to consult with others on the Board and elsewhere as to who was chosen. I went out of my way to see to it that all of the other panelists (who change somewhat every year—to keep the program fresh) had skills as editors and, usually, were also writers (we have always leaned towards selecting past winners of the Minnesota Voices Project), were open to new literature, and were independent-minded—often fiercely so.

The winning manuscripts were certainly not always my own top choice. (This was certainly true during the MVP panel session which took place on 1 November 1998.) If someone were to ask any of the panelists who have served over the years whether they felt in any way restricted in their own preferences and had been put on the panel to rubber-stamp my own choices, I strongly doubt that any of them would support such allegations. The judging sessions have always been lively, sometimes contentious, and truly democratic.

I mention this here in this context because I consider that the Minnesota Voices Project has always reflected a broad consensus in the winning choices made. This would not be true if the program were, in any way, founder-driven—certainly not in the seventeen-year history of the MVP.

4) While I have frequently been involved in editing some of our anthologies—most notably as co-editor of the series of three North American women traveling anthologies, in *Two Worlds Walking* (a col-

lection of writing by members of two or more national heritages), in *Talking of Hands* (our anthology for the Thirtieth Anniversary of New Rivers), and in a collection of North American prose poems called *The Party Train* (both co-edited by Robert Alexander, Mark Vinz, and myself)—I have certainly not been directly involved in any of the Many Minnesota Project's series of ethnic anthologies, of *Stiller's Pond*, the many collections in our New Rivers Abroad series, in the four anthologies in the *American Fiction* series (edited by Alan Davis and Michael White), in *Border Crossings*—a collection of writing from the states of Minnesota and the three prairie provinces of Canada (co-edited by Dave Williamson and Mark Vinz and co-published by Turnstone Press in Winnipeg), or in our collection of plays in *Slant Six*. While I always read the material selected and frequently make minor or even substantive suggestions to their editors, those have been free to make their own selections. They were chosen to edit such anthologies because of their own particular expertise and, in the case of the Many Minnesotas Project anthologies, they were members of the ethnic group being anthologized. Each of them had been carefully instructed in the history of New Rivers and its commitment to the publication of quality writing by new and emerging writers. And *Stiller's Pond*—a collection of short stories from the Upper Midwest—was co-edited by three short story writers (Jonis Agee, Roger Blakely, and Susan Welch) whom I knew would have different slants on literature because we wanted a provocative anthology. The Many Minnesotas Project series—unlike the Minnesota Voices Project, which was wholly conceived by me—grew out of a discussion I had with Jonis Agee and a fund-raising consultant for New Rivers, Vera Trent in 1982 or 1983.

5) Since New Rivers Press became a Federal 501(c)3 non-profit organization in 1982, it ceased to be owned by me. Essentially, control was transferred to the Board of Directors. I also stepped down as chairperson of the press in 1988 and became a non-voting member ten years later. Our first non-staff, non-paid chair was Richard Broderick. He was succeeded by John Mihelic, David Haynes, Gordon Thomas, and finally by Robert Alexander. The make-up of the Board has shifted, too. While writers continue to play an important role on it—Mark Vinz, David Vinz, David Haynes, Robert Alexander, and Julie Landsman—such non-writers as Deb Grossfield, Kathryn Bergstrom, Greg Danz, Michelle Woster, and Gordon Thomas now play an increasingly important role in determining the activities of the press. In the past ten years the Board of Directors has become much more active and now controls the organization.

6) But the main reason for carrying on New Rivers Press long after I am no longer connected with the organization is that its mis-

sion—first articulated by me—will continue to be an extremely important, even urgent, one. It was become alarmingly clear in recent years that the opportunities for writers of first books have shrunken dramatically—so much so that America, were it not for organizations like New Rivers, would have long since ceased to be a strong producer of first-rate literature.

It should be clear from these six points that while I have certainly been a strong and innovative force for New Rivers since its founding in 1968, it is not by any means a "founder-driven organization." It has long been my practice, especially in the past twenty years, to involve a great many individuals in everything we have done, individuals of strong mind and independent views whose contributions to the press have been immense and substantive. It pleases me to no end that I have been at the center of this for so long now, but New Rivers has flourished not only because of that drive on my part, through major difficulties, but because of the commitment of a great many other individuals to our mission and purposes. We continue to produce first-rate new books by emerging writers, often at the expense of greater sales. There is no evidence that this practice will not continue to govern the organization. And I see no reason why those commitments should not continue long into the future.

Non Profit Foreign Corporation Certificate of Authority from the Minnesota Department of State, 4 February 1977. C.W. Truesdale Papers (MSS77), University of Minnesota Libraries, Minneapolis, MN.

JOYCE SUTPHEN

The Poem You Said You Wouldn't Write

The poem you said you wouldn't write
is the one that I find myself reading this

morning, and even though I should be doing
something else, I find that I can't help writing

this poem about the sunlit patterns falling across
my desk, the sounds of cars starting up

in the neighborhood, and how it helps
to have these poems from you, the evidence

of things unseen, the substance of hope
that there will always be someone—the boy

sitting out on the front step with his transistor
radio, listening to news about Fidel Castro, or

the man sitting in his green lawn chair
watching how sky can be emptied of leaf,

branch, and trunk, until nothing is left
but stump and sawdust and your poem

about the tree, the one you said you wouldn't
write, the one that holds the branches high.

Focus

ALAN DAVIS

Author and editor, Alan Davis has had a decades-long relationship with New Rivers Press. He co-edited the American Fiction Series, *was twice an MVP winner, and was key to bringing the press to MSUM at the turn of the century. He serves now as senior editor and co-director.*

Duende and Efficiency: Working for Our Literary Ancestors and Ourselves

I moved to the flat, fertile Red River Valley of Minnesota from the undulating Piedmont of North Carolina in 1985 with my wife and one-year-old daughter to teach at Moorhead State University (now Minnesota State University Moorhead). I had written a collection of stories while pursuing a doctorate in literature and creative writing. By 1985, I had rewritten the collection, added to it and subtracted from it, and published stories in literary quarterlies. I felt confident enough to submit it to the various contests that I was only beginning to notice.

Since one of my colleagues in Minnesota was Mark Vinz, I became aware of Minneapolis-based New Rivers Press, where Vinz published and edited books and served irregularly as a member of their Board of Directors, and of New Rivers' founder and cantankerous guiding light, C.W. "Bill" Truesdale. At some point, I became aware that New Rivers held an annual competition open to writers who resided in several upper midwestern states, including Minnesota. I entered the contest, more than once, and would receive a detailed letter from Bill praising my work—close but no cigar—until 1992, when my collection, *Rumors from the Lost World*, was one of the titles chosen for publication. Bill appointed Vivian Vie Balfour, his wife, as my editor, and my meetings with her and with him were amicable, despite Bill's reputation as a difficult man, though he would swear me to secrecy about his smoking when we met without Vivian. She had wrung a promise from him that he wouldn't smoke—heart trouble—and he had no intention of keeping to that promise. Vivian, sniffing the air, would give me a look. "Was Bill smoking, Al?" I would give her a grin with my head tilted, and then frown, "Never mind about that, Vivian. This entire restaurant smells like a smokestack. Did my rewrites work for you?"

My book was published in 1993, with advance comments from Walker Percy, a mentor who died before the book found a publisher, and Tim O'Brien, who made my day by calling it "a magical collection of fiction, one of the best I've encountered in years." Armed with prepublication praise from *Kirkus Reviews* and *Publisher's Weekly* and *Booklist* and a glowing full-page review by Dorothy Allison in *The New York Times Book Review*, I was joyful—a writer with a well-received first book. It took me a year or more to understand that a small literary press like New Rivers wasn't in a position to take advantage of such a review and that Bill hated New York literary culture and wasn't much interested in their cultural organs. Besides, he had switched distributors shortly before the publication of my book and the former distributor, rumor had it, routinely told booksellers that New Rivers was kaput. That, at least, was Bill's way of telling me why nothing much happened for the book after the initial flurry of reviews. It was my welcome to the world of New Rivers Press.

***

By 2000, I had co-edited four editions of *American Fiction*, a national anthology, for the press. Since Michael C. White and I solicited manuscripts, screened them, hired a finalist judge, and delivered a book that was publication-ready, there were never any conflicts with Bill, who was pleased that the book sold better than many of his other titles. By the time I published a second collection, *Alone with the Owl*, also an MVP winner, with New Rivers, Bill Truesdale was sick and the press was in financial trouble. The last book published by the "old" New Rivers was Debra Marquart's *The Hunger Bone: Rock and Roll Stories*, fictionalized versions of her life as a female rock-and-roll singer. Debra still likes to say that the publication of her book was the final straw that put the press under.

In early 2001, I received a letter, as did all New Rivers authors and editors, informing us that the press was going into suspension due to Bill and Executive Director Phyllis Jendro's health and other difficulties. The letter told us personally what the industry learned shortly thereafter in *Publisher's Weekly* (on February 26, 2001, two days before Truesdale passed away):

> Minneapolis-based literary nonprofit New Rivers Press has suspended operations after 32 years. In announcing the deci-

sion, interim executive director Lisa Bullard cited a "series of calamities" that included distribution and production snags, heavy returns, and medical problems faced by founder C.W. Truesdale and executive director Phyllis Jendro.

The article mentioned that New Rivers had published more than three hundred titles, including works by Charles Simic, Charles Baxter, and David Haynes. "A lot of the challenges we faced were the result of industry-wide factors," Bullard said. "But when coupled with some of our other problems, we simply didn't have enough cushion to sustain blow after blow. New Rivers has always operated near the edge—that's the nature of small press publishing—but without big marketing budgets, it's difficult to sell regional and emerging writers, and we were reluctant to change our mission."

The article went on to say that Bullard was exploring possible partnerships with other nonprofit publishers, and would do what she could to help authors under contract find alternative publishers if necessary.

The idea of "possible partnerships" took hold of my imagination. I walked a few blocks under concrete skies to Atomic Coffee, a comfortable gathering place with exposed brick and a very slurpy-sounding espresso machine, to brood about the situation. My colleagues Wayne Gudmundson—a gifted landscape photographer who produced annual books of photographs by his mass communications students—and Lin Enger, also a fellow creative writer, were deep in conversation, so much so that I decided to sit by myself, but Wayne waved me over. "I got some bad news," I said. "New Rivers Press is out of business." They stared at me when I mentioned the word *partnership*. "You won't believe what we were just talking about," Lin said. He was so gangly then that he looked like he might slide like maple syrup out of his chair, and everything he said he said calmly. "Starting a press here in Moorhead." I did a double take and Wayne laughed. "He's not kidding." Wayne, like Lin, is tall, but he carries his weight differently. He's grounded, a methodical problem-solver with an Icelandic heritage, a deadpan grin, and a prankster's sense of humor. "He's really not kidding," he repeated.

Though Lin eventually decided not to be involved so that he would have more time for his own writing, Wayne and I devoted a great deal of time and energy toward convincing both the New Rivers Board of Directors in Minneapolis and our administrative supervisors and respective colleagues in Moorhead that bringing New Rivers to MSUM would be a good thing. Internally, we had to negotiate terms, such as the amount of reassigned time each of us would receive, where the press would be physically housed, and where inventory might be kept, and what kind of relationship we would have legally with the university. Externally, the university system honchos in the Twin Cities (Minneapolis and St. Paul, Minnesota) had to approve such an arrangement, and the New Rivers Press board likewise had to choose our proposal from among the several that were submitted. I thought more than once that Bill Truesdale, big and shambling and intuitively subversive of any organization, even his own press, must be howling in his grave.

We consulted with dozens of people, including the Minnesota Attorney General's office, and the pieces fell into place. We would relinquish our 501(c)3 designation (one of the oldest such designations in the country for a literary press) and be a part of the university, which itself is a nonprofit, of course. The university's Foundation would be our fund-raising arm to certify tax-deductible contributions. We would find the money to acquire, publish, and market books and would have editorial independence. The university would house us—somewhere—and store our inventory—somewhere else.

In return, we promised to involve as many students in the operations of the press as possible, to be a teaching press. Wayne had long been involved with students in book production, and I had long worked with others as an editor and writing instructor, so he and I divided duties—he would be director, I would be senior editor—and gave ourselves a year to get the "wheel of New Rivers" turning before publishing again. The McKnight Foundation, long a New Rivers funder, greased the wheel with a grant that helped retire the press's debt, a generous donation that made the revival possible, since the university made it clear to us, and reasonably so, that they wouldn't take on the press if it came with debt. We also promised New Rivers that we would publish the titles that they had in press unless an author under contract found another publisher in the meantime.

We did just that. Astonishingly, the scheme worked. In 2003, the first several titles, after various stumbles, rolled off the press. That spring, we published *Nice Girls* by Cezarija Abartis, a collection of stories, and two collections of poems, *Mozart's Carriage* by Daniel Bachhuber and *Paper Boat* by Cullen Bailey Burns. In the fall, we published two more books: *The Volunteer*, poems by Candace Black, and *Landing Zones,* stories by Ed Micus. The latter two titles were designed in-house, though all five had been selected by the "old" press. We celebrated and brought the authors to town to launch their books, but we also quickly came to understand that trying to publish books twice a year, given our teaching responsibilities, would be impossible. So we dovetailed our curriculum to the publishing industry calendar and decided to limit ourselves to a fall publication schedule.

Our list is a distinguished one. We still emphasize the work of new and emerging writers, many of them wonderfully accomplished, but we also publish writers in mid-career or late-career whose work either hasn't received the attention it deserves or whose former publishers, for marketing or other reasons, have decided to emphasize other (often younger) writers. We reprinted Richard Hoffman's *Half the House*, for example, a profound and controversial literary memoir that his New York publisher allowed to go out of print, which would have been a crime against literature.

As Wayne and I learned the ropes of literary publishing—what was possible and what wasn't—students came and went, mostly as interns or volunteers, many of them very talented as graphic designers or editors or marketing fellows or as gals or guys Friday who learned along with us. Some provided technical expertise that we didn't have, others enthusiasm. Some earned their credits and moved on; others became fast friends and colleagues who still work with us many years later. Even though we were housed on a university campus, we managed to create a workplace where *duende* was as significant as efficiency. Occasionally a student with a rigid personality structure would complain that we were mad geniuses, or worse, but we got things done, though sometimes just barely. Students helped us with day-to-day operations, enjoyed the fruits of their labors at our annual literary festival, where they had the opportunity to meet the writers whose books they had helped bring into the world, and met deadlines. (We tell our students that they can't take an "incomplete," because New Rivers is a small business with a product that must be produced on time.) Some of them work today in the publishing industry.

Now we offer a Certificate in Publishing that includes two publishing classes, one an introduction and the other a practicum. On the ISBN page of each book, we continue to list not only the usual cataloguing data but also the names of the various students who have designed, edited, and otherwise helped bring the book to press. A student looking for work has a calling card: "I designed this book," she can say to a prospective employer. "I co-edited this book, worked with its national distributor, and helped market it," he can brag. Allen Sheets, our art director, assigns a graphic designer to each book, and a book team of students from our MFA, English, and mass communications programs edits each title under the direction of our managing editor, Suzzanne Kelley, who lived for years in Alaska and has both a doctorate in history and experience teaching grade school. She runs a tight ship, in other words, but she also invites all and sundry to join us on Wednesdays for a pot of homemade soup, often flavored with wild game that her husband brought to ground. Under her guidance, and with the assistance of the university administration, the press has been fully integrated into the curriculum.

Some of our students are well versed in the fine arts while others cut their teeth as book team members who learn that literary editing is not simply a matter of applying the *Chicago Manual of Style* to a given text. Though authors who work with such teams don't gather anecdotes like the ones that Charles Baxter shares with us elsewhere in this book, they generally enjoy interacting with students who are usually passionate in their commitment to the work. Duende again. At the 2011 Association of Writers & Writing Programs convention, for example, Suzzanne and I met with Clint McCown, whose novel, *Haints,* was published the next fall. Clint, a rangy brown-haired Southerner and former actor who favors plaid shirts and a trimmed beard and now lives on a horse farm in Virginia, praised his book team, which was music to our ears, but he was also gleeful about the way the team, composed mostly of Midwesterners, tried to change his Southernisms to standard English. The title of his book (a Southern colloquialism for ghost, apparition, or lost soul) was their first challenge. They rose to it, and the three of us were delighted to sit in a hotel bar talking about what we talk about when we talk about New Rivers books. We still do our best to honor Truesdale's progressive spirit by publishing work with a strong sense of place that speaks to our troubled times with *satyagraha* (the truth force), empathy, and aesthetic courage. When I look at the list of titles that we've published since the revival, I believe that we've done that: Rachel Coyne's *Whiskey Heart* is Minnesota's answer to Daniel Woodrell's *Winter's Bone*; in *Mortar and Pestle,* Lisa Gill writes eloquently and metaphorically about herbal remedies and the aftermath of her diagnosis of MS; *Downriver People* by the late Bea Exner Liu is a haunting story about an American who lived through the Japanese invasion of China from 1935-1945. I'd be happy, if I had the time, to sit down right now and reread each of the books that we've published. Readers who are new to the press and its unique list are in for a treat.

***

We like to say that the "wheel of NRP" moves along three roads. Each fall, we begin the process of acquiring books that will go into production the following year, publish books we accepted the previous year, and work closely with our authors to market both our front list and backlist titles. As any small press publisher will tell you, the budget is always a preoccupation. Fiona McCrae, of Graywolf Press, once said to a group of us learning about the industry that "the more books you sell, the more money you lose." It made little sense to me at the time.

Now, it seems like common sense. If she was joking, the joke now works for me like a Zen *koan*. It relieves tension on those days when red ink is on the rise.

Elsewhere in this book, you'll read about production and fund-raising and marketing. Here, my job is to tell you how we acquire books and how we work with them once we have them. Like many literary presses, we find books in four ways: We have an annual competition, our Many Voices Project (MVP), for new and emerging writers in both prose and poetry; we read (in May and occasionally otherwise) over-the-transom (unsolicited) submissions; we solicit manuscripts from writers whose work we discover or admire, and often work with a New Rivers author on another book; and we contract with editors to produce anthologies. Frequently these days, we also receive queries from agents, despite the fact that we have little financial incentive to offer someone representing an author. Elizabeth Searle's wonderful novel, *Girl Held in Home*, which we published in 2011, was agented, as was Clint McCown's *Haints*. In a better culture, such novels would be wildly sought out by major commercial publishers and promoted everywhere. We're delighted to have them and to publish them, because they're quirky and literary as well as accessible, and to do what we can for them, but the fact that neither Searle nor McCown had any luck finding a commercial publisher is evidence of mainstream lassitude.

I'm telling you that these two novels are written by established writers who have arrived, not by new or emerging ones. Bill almost always published first and second books and authors like Charles Baxter or Charles Simic or David Haynes, who would then move on to a different publisher, or maybe Bill would lose interest when a writer had *emerged*—whatever that means in today's culture. (Tobias Wolff, in his introduction as finalist judge to an issue of *American Fiction* some years ago, wrote that an emerging writer is any writer who is not guaranteed the certainty of publication elsewhere. By that definition, *emerged* writers are few and far between.) Likewise, several years ago we published *Flock and Shadow: New and Selected Poems* by Michael Hettich, a Florida poet who is among the dozen or fifteen or twenty poets currently at work in the United States whose work matters most. He's essential, that is, not emerging, but New Rivers published him, and we'll continue to look for such writers who are not being served by either the mainstream publishers or the larger literary presses.

Even so, New Rivers Press is still best known for its attention to new and emerging writers. Our MVP competition solicits manuscripts each fall by placing ads in *Poets & Writers* and *Writers' Chronicle*, among other trade magazines. We receive, on average, six hundred book-length manuscripts, approximately half of them poetry and half prose. In the past, when the competition was regional (Minnesota, North Dakota, South Dakota, Wisconsin, and Iowa), Bill, I've been told, would corral a group of writers to read every submission and meet with them in the Twin Cities to hash out contest winners, According to anecdote, the decisions were made with pizza and camaraderie (nobody got western) but without democracy, since Bill sometimes knew what he wanted and insisted that others should consider wanting the same thing. It was his press, after all. Sometimes, that's the way it used to work, and perhaps reasonably so—one man's vision might keep such an operation shambling along year after year, and the books Bill published could surprise and astonish. Bill's stamp of approval was attached to every one.

Suzzanne Kelley and Alan Davis marvel at all the manuscript submissions arriving for the Many Voices Project competition, 2009. Photo by Nancy Swan.

Now we do it differently. We have a finalist judge in poetry and almost always another in prose (unless a given judge has published notable books in multiple genres and is willing to do double duty). Each judge receives anywhere from eight to fifteen finalists, depending on genre and the recommendations of screeners. I coordinate prose screening and do a great deal of screening in prose, while my colleague, Kevin Carollo, does the same in poetry.

The screening itself takes months. Manuscripts are read and reread. Each manuscript receives a rating, ranging from one to five, and comments from each screener, who provides a summary, an overview, and a recommendation: a 1 is "A must keep for next round or editorial session. Knocks your socks off. Wow!"

Maurice Riordan, the poetry editor of *Poetry London* (Autumn 2005), mentions how Ford Madox Ford, who edited the *English Review*, was following "the melancholy routine of all editors," dropping submissions into the reject pile, when he came across "Odour of Chrysanthemums" by the unknown D. H. Lawrence. Wisely, he accepted it; it was Lawrence's first publication. Riordan writes: "I have been reminded of Ford's anecdote often this past summer, as I've sifted through my own pile of submissions. Is there a genius to be discovered in here? And then the worrying thought: What if there is and I should miss him or her? What made Ford so sure?" He answers his own question: While there are "qualities the attentive reader can recognize and linger over," a "subconscious response preceding active interest is what may save him from the ignominy of not seeing the hidden genius. . . . Emily Dickinson has often described this in physical terms—notoriously as having the top of her head blown off! Robert Graves had a more homely, if effectively gender specific, test for a true poem. He found when he recited the lines they caused the hairs to bristle on his chin. Doing so before the mirror helped him with his morning shave." Such discoveries, needless to say, are few and far between, but it's one of the things every editor lives for.

Unfortunately, teaching a screener to recognize genius, even if I'm fortunate enough to recognize it myself, is an art, not only a craft, that depends on long experience making such evaluations. I sometimes point out, when I disagree with a ranking, that in the late '80s I helped to pay the bills while my wife earned a second college degree by reviewing more than five hundred titles for *Kirkus Reviews* and other periodicals. One learns to be succinct and instantaneous without making snap judgments, the way a baseball player in the majors learns to hit by swinging a bat thousands of times and making contact often enough to keep his average at least respectable.

It's easier to explain the criteria that come into play to rank a submission as a 2: "Consider further. Original, convincing. Language serves the material and often surprises with its aptness or metaphorical precision. Problems or reservations (expressed above) are minor, and could be fixed with careful editing." All of these submissions also make it to the next round of reading, whereas a submission ranked 3 ("Competent material, well-crafted but uninspiring. Little distinguishes it from fifty other such manuscripts. Reject but encourage writer to try us again."), doesn't. Such submissions are a common sight in the age of workshops: Promising but not yet ripe. As for 4 ("Weak manuscript with too many flaws. Doesn't go anywhere. The language is either flat or too often incorrect. Some clunkers and obvious clumsiness. OR—genre material, inappropriate for NRP.") and 5 ("Weak manuscript that's amateurish or otherwise inappropriate for NRP. Reading past the first few pages becomes a waste of time."), the less said about them, the better.

Any screener can recommend a manuscript for the next round. By the end of the process, our heads are swirling and we're elated to have found a suitable number of publishable manuscripts and unhappy to think that we might have missed one that should be a finalist. (A number of writers, of course, withdraw their submissions during the process because they've found another publisher in this age of multiple submissions.) It's an imperfect process, but each year the two judges invariably praise the finalists and often find more than one title to recommend.

We then think about those other finalists and whether we would like to offer to publish any of them as a general submission. I'm always aware that we're limited at present to publishing six titles a year. We want a mixture of genres, if possible. We have several anthologies in the pipeline this year, for example, but none of them are ready to publish next year. In the past, New Rivers published works in translations, or works from abroad by American writers, in the New Rivers Abroad series, and Kevin Carollo, who's the editor of that series, is trying to find suitable titles. I also have received a number of manuscripts, some of them over-the-transom, some of them solicited, to consider for publication. At the AWP, for example, several authors promised me manuscripts, and I look forward to receiving and reading them during our open submission process. Also, several New Rivers authors have new, promising books that we'd like to publish if we can find a spot for them.

The acquisition process is both methodical and helter-skelter at a small literary press without a full-time editor. The writer James Dickey, I've read, was a diabetic who some days would decide whether to eat or to drink; many days, I have to decide whether to read the worthy work of others or devote time to my own work-in-progress. My MFA colleagues sometimes volunteer to help sort through submissions. Thom Tammaro, for example, is our poetry editor, but he's unpaid, so I'm careful when I ask him for his time and energy. He covered for me when I was on sabbatical several years ago, and that year co-edited (with Joyce Sutphen, Minnesota's current poet laureate, and Connie Wanek) *To Sing Along the Way: Minnesota Women Poets from Pre-Territorial Days to the Present*, one of our best-selling titles and an invaluable addition to our list. (We have a house rule, by the way: Colleagues can propose anthologies as editors, but we don't consider their own books for publication, to avoid a conflict of interest and migraine headaches.)

I'm currently reading a novel that I like. That might be the novel we'll put on next year's list, though I have several others to read before making a decision. I don't know what might arrive in the mail or via e-mail. (For our MVP competition, we used to require only hard copies sent through the regular mail; now we also accept online submissions via the website Submittable. For *American Fiction,* we accept either hard copies or stories submitted online. I don't use the web for general submissions, but I'm agreeable to e-mail submissions, so long as a writer queries me first and gives me an opportunity to reply.) I do know that we have two slots reserved on next year's list for the MVP winners; a third slot intended for a novel that will change the consciousness of the world; a fourth for either another novel, a collection of stories, or a nonfiction submission; and probably the final two slots will be two books of poems. It will all come out in the wash, as my mom liked to say. We always have more books we'd like to publish than we can afford to acquire. Bill Truesdale could accept twenty titles if he wished and go into debt. We can't—the university would drop us if we were fiscally irresponsible or took unacceptable risks. Some small-press publishers in the past century were cowboys or divas who did as they pleased. Stories about them make for wonderful cultural memoirs that I love to read or hear. When NRP authors get together, many of them have "Bill" stories that they love to share. They're wonderful stories.

Bill published many notable anthologies—a Vietnam anthology (*The Perimeter of Light*), an anthology of writers of mixed heritage (*Two Worlds Walking*), anthologies by American women living or traveling abroad (*Tanzania on Tuesday, An Inn Near Kyoto*), Irish-American (*The Next Parish Over*), Slovak-American (*The Boundaries of Twilight*), *Poems from Italy* edited by Dana Gioia and William Jay Smith, and a prose poem anthology (*The Party Train*). We're more selective, given our resources and constraints, but I've already mentioned the Minnesota women poet anthology, *To Sing Along the Way. American Fiction* is biennial, and we're preparing volume thirteen for publication next fall, so that won't be on next year's list of acquisitions, but there is a fifth category of titles that we occasionally publish: those that we choose in partnership with other nonprofits. *Duane Hanson: Portraits from the Heartland,* for example, is a title that is a gallery catalog that offers a major new perspective and reappraisal of the photorealist sculptor; we published it in collaboration with the Plains Art Museum. In 2007, we partnered with the Stonecoast low-residency MFA program to offer a book prize to writers associated with that program; finalist judge Katha Pollitt selected Penelope Schwartz Robinson's *Slippery Men*, a collection of essays, as the winner. Likewise, we partnered with the Fairfield University low-residency MFA program in Connecticut to offer a similar prize, and finalist judge Charles Simic selected Nick Knittel's *Good Things*, a collection of stories that was published fall 2012. We live in an era of diminishing resources in our industry, and we believe that partnering with Minnesota State

University Moorhead as a teaching press and with other organizations when possible on select titles benefits all of us.

***

When I look in the mirror, I don't see Bill Truesdale. I've never called myself Doctor Vertigo, the title of his own self-published book of poems with his clean-shaven kindly photograph on the front cover. (By contrast, when I knew Bill, in the '90s, he was grizzled, his high-pitched voice somehow at odds with his physical persona, which, despite his pale skin, reminded me of a medium-sized black bear that can be found in tourist traps in the Black Hills of South Dakota.) What I do see, however, is yet another person doing what he can to keep literature alive, not in any abstract sense, but by discovering and publishing the best work of every character that comes to my attention. I think that all of us at New Rivers feel that way. Given our resources, it's a modest effort, but the result can be measured not only by the body of work, the books we publish each year and the praise that they receive, but also by the many transient students and volunteers who work with us, learn some things about the publishing trade and the worth of books, and carry that lore with them when they graduate.

Literary small presses are tenuous things; they last, sometimes, but they also come and go like fireflies. In a culture where crony capitalism, competitive athletics, and entertainment trump art at almost every turn, there's something noble and quixotic about our endeavor. Many thousands of us are passionate to the point of mild insanity about what we like or dislike, about our aesthetic preferences and intellectual tastes and the choices that we make when we choose a book to read, or a story to tell if we're writers, but it's still possible to say, despite the clockwork nature of our society, that we're all Bill Truesdale, searching for the one true word. Langston Hughes pointed out that society would just as soon kill a genius child "—and let his soul run wild." Literary small presses, if they're doing their job, nurture such voices. New Rivers Press is a place for writers to come home to.

At the same time, we all have a business to run. This year, New Rivers has produced its new prose titles not only in beautiful print editions but also as eBooks available at Amazon, barnesandnoble.com, and elsewhere, and has begun the project of making backlist titles available in digital formats. We have a lively Facebook page that's featured on our website. We've begun to use social media and blogs to promote our authors and keep our readers informed about deadlines and other items of interest. Suzzanne spends a great deal of time at AWP focused on the business of small-press publishing. The wildness we crave and nurture can't survive for long without structure, but structure without innovation, improvisation, and wildness becomes stultifying bureaucracy that snuffs out creativity.

Why do we persevere in the face of cultural indifference, slovenliness, and amnesia? I think it's because we're working not only for ourselves and the beings who inhabit the earth with us, but also for the invisible guests, our literary ancestors. They hover in our slipstreams the way a peregrine falcon, which has been clocked at two hundred miles per hour during its high-speed hunting swoop, hovers high above the earth until it finds its prey. We sit alone amidst piles of manuscripts and the eureka moment arrives—like Ford Madox Ford happening upon the unknown D. H. Lawrence, we forget the backaches and the eyestrain. Something is happening—again. Someone's voice is speaking to us—again. The ego opens its petals and forgets to be lonely. We listen, and our ancestors come close. They listen, too.

JOYCE SUTPHEN

How I See the World

In color, just like I dream, and always
gratefully, though perhaps I often seem
distracted. (I am, aren't you?)

I see it in voices coming to me
on the radio, in the telephone,
and on the wind. I hear it in the words

I read on the page, I see it in time—
one of us being born and the other
dying. Spring and Fall—both at once.

Death (whatever that is). I can't see it,
but how I love the way that leaf (just now
when I looked up) floated down from the tree

so slowly, taking its time—all the time
in the world—for me to see it falling.

DONNA CARLSON

Donna Carlson served as managing editor for seven years, easing the press's transition into its role as a nonprofit, literary teaching press. She has since retired to live near family in Connecticut.

New Rivers Press:
New Beginnings at MSUM

*B*oxes of files and published books from Minneapolis arrived at the Minnesota State University Moorhead campus in 2002, and work began during the summer with volunteers, Athena Gracyk and Rebecca West, assisting Wayne Gudmundson and Alan Davis in unpacking and organizing materials. In the fall semester, the process—completing the editing and production of three works under contract with New Rivers Press before its move to MSUM—began.

***

That was New Rivers Press when I began helping for a few hours a week in January 2003—many departments, faculty, and students, working as a team to get three books out in the spring of that year, while at the same time trying to set up, organize, and run an office.

I had come to publishing obliquely and on a meandering path, arriving at New Rivers Press when the first three books were in the last stages of editing. But my interest in books started long before.

"Donna June, go outside and play. You always have your nose in a book." I can still hear my mother's disapproving voice. In the 1920s, she had lived in a children's home in London, England, where personal worth was measured by the quality and amount of work accomplished in a day. But that was then and, while I didn't mind work when I was growing up, I also longed to read. When jet planes were a less common sight in our skies than now, friends and I would stop play, look up and exclaim, "Look! It's a jet! Look at the jet stream!" and stand amazed at the sound and speed of the plane. Where was that jet going? Who was on it? What was the inside of the plane like?

Stories and books were my jet plane: They took me to exciting places, to experiences I could only imagine in my real life, the fifth of six children in our family, living on the corner of 9th and Washington streets in the small city of Jamestown, New York.

And words—how fascinating words were. At the age of six or so when I was learning to read, I sat next to my father reading to him. When a word stumped me, I tried sounding it out—"Ree-lay´-tiv, reel´-a-tive, ree-, rel´-, rel-a-tive, it's relative!" I beamed and my dad smiled as I remembered my parents' word for extended family—our relatives. So the word "relative" set me on a course of infatuation with and love for words. In high school, Latin provided an introduction to the derivation of many English words and to the beauty of language; college English courses taught the struggles and stories behind the history of the English language; and a semester of study and travel in Belgium and Europe brought artists' stories to life, and showed the scars, heroics, tragedies, and engineering ingenuity of Roman occupation that influenced the history and language of Europe. First year Latin's story of Caesar's crossing the Rubicon, of Hannibal's march over the Pyrenees and Alps with war elephants, became reality; it was all more than just a fascinating story—it had really happened.

Words and stories seemed magical, and those strands of imagination continued through my life as mother, then museum curator, into teaching art history, and then into publishing and editing. Stories are the blocks of human life. Mid-20th-century Georgia writer Raymond Andrews said in a 1988 *Albany Review* interview: "I don't know how to make a plot; I just tell a story. I say hell, life's got no plot. But it's sure full of characters" ("Raymond Andrews [1934–91]: The County as Heart, History, and Universe [an introduction]," by Stephen Corey and Douglas Carlson, *The Georgia Review*, Fall 2010, p. 393). When I read that quote I understood, and I thought of all the authors' stories and characters I'd worked with in the past seventeen years.

Not until working in the mid-1990s with Dennis Maloney and Elaine LaMattina at White Pine Press, a literary small press founded by Maloney just four years after Truesdale founded New Rivers Press, did I understand the conflux of words, stories, and fine writing. Good writing is transformational in transmitting authors' sensory experiences and the world of their imaginations to readers; their works can change lives. And small publishing houses are a perfect platform for getting emerging work to a larger audience. Small presses have the luxury of being able to spend time on and pay attention to their work. Elaine LaMattina was (and still is) one of the most talented editors in small press publishing. She taught me about author-press relationships and many other facets of publishing and editing in the three years of work with Dennis and her before I moved to Minnesota in 1997.

***

In preparation for proposing New Rivers' move to campus, Gudmundson and Davis had talked with and/or communicated with other small literary presses in Minnesota and other parts of the country. What they were venturing into was a specialized world of a small group of nonprofit publishers that focused on recognizing and publishing fine writing by little-known literary artists. Recognizing the specialty of the project, they sought advice and suggestions from similar successful organizations such as Milkweed Editions, Coffee House Press, and Graywolf Press, all based in Minneapolis. Among others contacted outside of Minnesota was Elaine LaMattina at White Pine Press, who suggested that Gudmundson and Davis contact me.

I had learned the basics at White Pine—book production, editing, publishing, promotion, distribution, and working with a book distributor: Consortium Book Sales and Distribution, the same small press distributor that New Rivers Press had chosen. Located in a college town, White Pine Press brought in college students as interns, and I had worked closely with them.

Al Davis tracked me down—I was working as an adjunct instructor in the art department at the time—and, over drinks at the Red Bear, Wayne, Al, and I talked publishing. When they offered me part-time work with the press, the move seemed natural. I knew that Elaine and Dennis would be helpful whenever we had questions and that the publishing experience would be similar to that at White Pine Press. It was the beginning of what became a strong publishing team and a successful teaching and publishing venture.

***

As I sit at my desk in Connecticut, nearly 1,800 miles from Moorhead and MSUM, I glance up at the New Rivers Press books on my bookshelf, arranged alphabetically by author for each MSUM publishing cycle for ten years beginning in 2003—spring 2003: Abartis, Cezarija, *Nice Girls and Other Stories*; Bachhuber, Daniel, *Mozart's Carriage*; Burns, Cullen Bailey, *Paper Boat*—each publishing cycle similarly arranged.

Each title and author up to 2010 (when I moved to Connecticut) conjures memories of working with the student book teams and designers of the books, and of working with authors—finally meeting them and being able to associate a face and personality with the name on e-mails and the voice at the other end of phone conversations, the person behind the imagination that created the books on the shelf.

With each book, I realized how much New Rivers had evolved from its beginnings at MSUM, how writing had changed (or not) in ten years. I pondered the changes the organization had gone through, and especially the technological advances reflected in the books' editing, printing, distribution, and sales—ten years of changing technology so rapid that they might be compared to the cultural and mechanical changes in the first *fifty* years of the twentieth century.

***

In those first years, New Rivers Press operated out of a number of office locations before settling into 243 Flora Frick Hall on the MSUM campus. In January 2003, the location was a vacant faculty office in McLean Hall, across from Gudmundson's office. Equipment—all recycled or borrowed—was sparse: a computer or two, a file cabinet, tables and chairs, a gray metal office desk shared by everyone who worked there at various times of the day in various capacities, and the necessary coffee pot. A work-study student, Charane Wilson, ran the office for about ten hours a week, becoming familiar with New Rivers' databases and files; and Timothy Litt, a volunteer, spent time developing the New Rivers website. Workers came and went, talking about books not published yet, sharing ideas for cover art, planning new projects, New Rivers' start. In spring 2003, my time with New Rivers was limited to about five hours a week. I remember, though, that the office almost vibrated with anticipation of what the organization might become; the atmosphere seemed charged with possibilities and buzzed with a promise of success.

By the end of the semester, graduate English students under Al's supervision had finished editing the three books scheduled for spring publication; book covers had been designed for the first publishing cycle by design companies in Minneapolis that had been preselected under Truesdale's leadership, so they were ready to go; a design team under Julie Mader-Meersman, professor in the Art Department, designed and set the interiors; the press had chosen a printer and sent files off. By May, the first three books hit the bookstores. Students who had worked on them read their names on the copyright pages and held the books in their hands, knowing that bookstores nationwide were stocking them and that Amazon.com and Barnes and Noble's BN.com had online preorders. And by May, three authors who, the year before, thought that their work might not be published, now saw their names on books being sold in bookstores and online:

Cezarija Abartis, Daniel Bachhuber, and Cullen Bailey Burns became the first authors published by New Rivers Press at Minnesota State University Moorhead. It was a time filled with excitement and amazement that this new and unique experimental adventure was working. People wanted to be a part of it.

Athena Gracyk, with help and funding from the MSUM Alumni Association, organized a celebration to launch the books at The Loft Literary Center in Minneapolis. Invitations went to all former New Rivers Press employees, boards of directors, Mrs. Truesdale, and all New Rivers authors. The featured authors read from their hot-off-the-press works. On that night, New Rivers Press demonstrated to its and Bill Truesdale's friends and colleagues that it would continue his vision and long history of publishing quality and original writing by emerging authors.

The theme of the event, "New Rivers Press Flows Again," became the New Rivers Press motto, and the event's poster design became the first stationery and business logo. The 2003 book launch also initiated the annual New Rivers Press Literary Festival, which continued for five years.

***

By fall semester of 2003, Gudmundson and Davis had succeeded in outlining requirements for a Certificate in Publishing. The keystone course was Introduction to Publishing, which met for the first time that semester. This course was designed to familiarize students with all facets of small press publishing, and New Rivers Press served as a working model and case study for concepts learned in class. Students learned from professionals in the publishing field the structure and business model of a small literary press; the history of the small press movement in the United States; how books are acquired and edited; copyright law; book design; fund-raising; and how books are promoted, marketed, and sold.

The semester's classroom work became concrete for students with a trip to the Twin Cities at the end of the semester. There at The Center for Book Arts, students saw hand-operated letterpresses and lead type, and saw how books are produced by hand, much like Truesdale's first attempts at publishing. The Loft Literary Center, in the same building, served as a space that promoted and encouraged working writers and maintained a library of small press publications and literary journals. Staff at other small literary presses such as Milkweed Editions or Coffee House Press explained the operations of small publishing houses similar to New Rivers Press.

Consortium Book Sales and Distribution, the New Rivers' book distributor, provided a tour of their facility, including the warehouse and "picking" center where books from all of Consortium's clients were shipped at that time. The numbers of "returns," that is, books not sold by certain stores during a given time period and contracted for return without penalty, drove home to students the tentative nature of any book sale. Many books came back to the distributor damaged beyond resale possibility, which meant monetary loss for both the distributor and the publisher—a valuable and indelible lesson for students hoping to enter the publishing business.

Students could draw interesting comparisons in book production between that at The Center for Book Arts and at BookMobile, a print-on-demand book producer that printed New Rivers Press books by computer.

Students from the spring 2013 Introduction to Publishing course study leading trays at the Minnesota Center for Book Arts. Photo by Suzzanne Kelley.

After the Introduction to Publishing course had been offered each semester for a while with student editorial book teams operating separately from class time, the staff realized that more time and consistency was needed for class members to become more fully a part of the editing process. The Practicum in Publishing course, offered for the first time in fall 2004, helped standardize the editing process and give students built-in time to edit as book teams and to exchange ideas, successes, and failures.

***

In the fall of 2003 the New Rivers Press office was moved from McLean Hall to 240 Frick Hall, a windowless, trapezoidal room with an area of possibly 100 square feet. A counter ran the length of the east wall, and the wider end of the trapezoid at the entrance provided just enough room for two four-drawer file cabinets. They filled quickly with author files as box after box from Minneapolis emptied—a good way for staff to become familiar with previous New Rivers authors and book titles.

That semester New Rivers Press restarted the Minnesota Voices Project (MVP) Contest, which had been suspended during the sale, acquisition, and move to MSUM. Shortly after the contest submission date, boxes of manuscripts lined the counter, then, as more entries arrived, filled the space beneath the counter, and on the floor along the opposite wall; all areas were stacked two or three boxes high by the deadline date. Only a patch of countertop remained for computer and workspace, and only a narrow path from door to rear wall provided access. It was clear that the press had already outgrown 240 Frick Hall.

Shortly afterward New Rivers moved its office next door to 243 Frick Hall where it remained until 2009. This office was far more spacious and workable than the previous one, with room for more computers, bookshelves, and additional file cabinets. As in 240 Frick, a counter ran along the east wall and, now, also the south wall, providing much-needed surface area for work. By this time, the staff understood that we needed to function as a successful business and, to do that, we needed to create a center of gravity for the press—a locus of operation—that would establish New Rivers' organizational DNA and get the word out. Uniformity and coordination of New Rivers' operation became a goal. This bigger office provided the physical space for necessary office equipment and room for student workers to learn while assisting the staff. The office became a center of constant activity.

Soon a copy of every New Rivers Press book published since 1968 that student assistants had been able to locate lined bookshelves along the south wall above the counter. The collection proved to be a study in small press technology, in publishing and literary changes and interests, and in changing cultural influences. Some books were first or early works by writers who later became nationally known, such as Charles Baxter, Albert Goldbarth, and Dana Gioia, poet and translator and former director of the National Endowment for the Arts.

What fun to open the books from the early 1970s and see reflected the experimental nonconformity of that decade—a looseleaf book in a box; books with hand drawings and sketches; vaguely veiled sexual allusions. Some books reflected a growing interest in the environment brought about by the first Earth Day in 1970. Over the decades New Rivers Press books reflected interest in women's issues, various personal identities sought and found, and Asian culture and translations.

The office at 243 Frick Hall had more space to accommodate the numerous boxes of manuscripts that continued to come in for the MVP Contest—its name changed to the Many Voices Project—with winners from places outside the Upper Midwest and one from Minnesota.

***

By the time the press moved into Frick 243, Wayne and Al had secured more hours for the part-time position of managing editor and hired me to fill the job. The managing editor ran the office, supervised student workers, acted as liaison and contact with Consortium Book Sales and Distribution, taught publishing classes, and worked with authors to help shepherd their work from submission to publication.

Much of our success depended on and came from the vital component of excellent student involvement. Students worked as editors on book teams and provided much-needed office assistance; they organized literary festivals, a time-consuming job requiring juggling many people and activities. Graphic design students under supervision of Allen Sheets, professor in the Art Department, designed posters, brochures, catalogs, and entire books. The MVP contest often attracted more than four hundred entries, and students worked long and hard in designing a login system for entries and in organizing the manuscripts in preparation for judging.

Students became involved in class projects necessary to New Rivers' operation. Among the projects completed were marketing specific books to targeted geographical areas (*Pilgrimage with Fish* to the Alexandria lakes region [Michelle Roers]); creating and designing the twenty-fifth anniversary MVP catalog (Brenda Davis); developing and editing the New Rivers Press newsletter (Gerri Stowman, Teresa Schafer); creating and implementing a marketing plan for *To Sing Along the Way, Minnesota Women Poets . . .* anthology (Suzzanne Kelley); shelving and organizing books at the Annex (Brett Ortler, Abbey Thompson, and others); creating reader's guides for many New Rivers books; and creating and editing a promotional DVD that provided an introduction to New Rivers Press in classes and at Association of Writers and Writing Programs (AWP) conferences (Jennifer Baaken).

Some students came to New Rivers through work-study or independent-study programs, some were Honors Apprentices or graduate and undergraduate interns, and others were volunteers. Every job or project on which students worked was essential or useful to our operation. Students often proposed and served on panels at AWP's national conferences, where they also helped set up and work at the book table.

A usual book team was comprised of four or five students who selected the manuscripts they would edit based on genre and staff descriptions. Each team chose someone who would be author contact, who would present the team's ideas and edits to the author. Book teams met on a regular basis to complete their edits according to Consortium's and New Rivers' publishing schedule. This was not just a class but the real world of publishing demands and deadlines necessary for getting the book printed on time. Each week in the Practicum class, book teams would present their progress, concerns, problems, or coups to the class for discussion. By the end of the semester book teams would have finished their edits, conferred with the authors, and finalized their preparations for the manuscripts to go to the book designers.

Working closely with students was one of the joys of the job of managing editor. Each semester, book teams worked diligently and grew professionally. Enthusiasm in the class increased as book teams shared their work with others in the class and with designers creating the book's visual image. All involved in the project sensed that they were participating in the community and shared purpose that New Rivers Press represents.

Each fall the staff anticipated meeting with new book designers, graphic design students selected by Allen Sheets, who brought extensive and highly acclaimed experience in book design to working with these students. Designers read the manuscripts for design ideas while the book teams were reading them for editorial suggestions. New Rivers Press staff—Wayne Gudmundson, Al Davis, Thom Tammaro, and I—first met with design students to see three possible cover designs, which they had created in consultation with Allen Sheets. The staff selected one design, for which students created three versions. After the cover design was selected, work began on the book's interior—typeface, type size, layout.

Cover designs were inevitably creative and thoughtful, sometimes complicated, sometimes minimalist. Since it's impossible to include all here, I'll mention three memorable covers. One features an image, in shades of red, of a fish head. During the photo shoot, the fish had been removed from its ice pack and photographed as the photographer's lights slowly melted the ice and released the reek of old, dead fish throughout the studio (Ed Bok Lee's *Real Karaoke People*, 2005, designed by Katie Elenberger, photographed by Bob Wimmer). The cover is evocatively striking and one of the most eye-catching of New Rivers' books. Another cover features a beautifully simple stalk of lavender on a light green ground (Diane Jarvenpa's *The Tender Wild Things*, 2007, designed by Sarah Teveldal), the suggestion of the fragrance of lavender (as opposed to the odor of old fish). The third cover conveys stark coldness: white ground, softened only by a warm blue outline of an Arctic wren (Kelsea Habecker's *Hollow Out*, 2008, designed by Angelina Lennington), reflecting the release that spring brings after the long Arctic winter described by the poems held in the book.

Every publication became a true team effort with book teams, authors, designers, and faculty contributing to the final book. With mutual respect and cooperation, all students involved contributed to a published product that each team member could claim—a point of pride. At AWP conferences people stopped at the table, often drawn to the book covers. Frequently they commented on the books' originality (without an "institutional" identifying style, they would note), impressed that they were student designs. Many book covers won national graphic design contests, an honor to the students and to MSUM's graphic design program.

***

Recently, as I left the public library where I live in Connecticut, I spotted a book on the withdrawn and sale shelves. For twenty-five cents I picked up a book by Jenna Blum, recognizing the author's name and the book title from soliciting a blurb from her in 2005. There in her acknowledgments Blum thanked Tricia Currans-Sheehan, editor of the *Bloomsburg Review,* for publishing the original story. Currans-Sheehan is a New Rivers Press author, and her 2006 book, *The River Road,* is the book that carries the Jenna Blum blurb solicited in 2005.

The experience reminded me of the excellent writing that New Rivers publishes, the extent of its sales and network, and the close contact our staff has with their authors. New Rivers Press is known for its working relationship between author and publisher. Mail often includes notes of gratitude from authors, thanking students and staff for help given them and their work. It's one of the most gratifying and enjoyable parts of being a part of the New Rivers community. Authors become friends that we socialize with each year at AWP conferences.

Our first personal contact with authors from 2003 through 2007 came with the New Rivers Press Annual Literary Festival, which was held each October and planned entirely by students—a huge undertaking. These dedicated and organized students scheduled readings, arranged venues, chose restaurants and menus, planned speakers, arranged for off-campus events, and wrote public announcements and advertising. Art students designed posters, invitations, and fliers. Banners made from book cover designs hung in the lobby of Owens Hall and at readings, and were carried to AWP and regional conferences. With apologies for naming so few students when so many did so much, these three deserve mention as literary festival coordinators who organized the literary festivals so well: Athena Gracyk (2003); Jill Haugen (2004); and Heather Steinmann (2005, 2006, 2007). Photos of authors (John Chattin, Diane Jarvenpa, Holaday Mason, and Purvi Shah, among others) meeting and talking with their books' designers and book teams at literary festivals are in the New Rivers Press photo archive.

***

Each Intro to Publishing and Practicum class ended the semester with a party of pizza and snacks and, at the end of the fall semester, holiday cookies. The Introduction to Publishing class in the spring of 2005 had bonded on the bus coming back from the Cities—songs and laughter made the trip back to Moorhead seem like a short ride to the mall. The end-of-semester party lasted for over an hour while classmates chatted and laughed and reminisced and planned. The food was gone, the semester was over, but still they enjoyed each other's conversations enough to stay into the evening. And from that fun class with lots of laughter came many good projects, including the MVP twenty-fifth anniversary catalog by Brenda Davis, who found all the books, scanned covers, and designed, wrote, and typeset the entire catalog over two semesters.

***

The Red River crested at a one-hundred-year-record forty-one-plus feet on March 28, 2009. Area classes and events had been cancelled the entire week to allow everyone to prepare and help others prepare for the impending flooding. Some parts of the Fargo-Moorhead area were evacuated. My house was in an evacuation zone. Wayne and Jane Gudmundson lived in the same section of the city but chose to stay and help people who needed it and check on vacant properties. Al and Cathy Davis lived on higher ground and weren't threatened but took in and in other ways helped people who were. That kind of community and shared purpose is a Fargo-Moorhead hallmark, and one that carried over to the New Rivers Press community.

***

New Rivers Press moved from the aegis of the Mass Communications Department to the English Department in 2008, and the office moved in 2009 to Weld 108, where it is today. This office is larger and far more practically laid out and serviceable as an office and meeting space (and it has windows to the outside!).

On September 30, 2009, I wrote my family on the East Coast: "Today we celebrated the inauguration of the new New Rivers Press office in a new office space in a new building under a new dean, and officially introduced Suzzanne Kelley, the new managing editor, to the college community. . . . I'll miss this organization, these people, this community, these plains and Badlands." When the semester ended, friends helped pack and load the moving truck. I filled the back seat and trunk of my Corolla with leftover more fragile belongings, placed a large Christmas cactus on the passenger seat, finished cleaning the house, then crammed the vacuum cleaner onto the floor of the back seat, the handle wedged between the front seats. Jane, Cathy, and I met one more time at Atomic Coffee, then, fighting back tears, I headed east, dodging lake-effects storms across seven Great Lakes states.

My role with New Rivers Press had ended, but the New Rivers Press organization continues to grow and evolve. The characters come and go, and the plot develops and redevelops. Weld 108 still serves as the hub of the organization, where Suzzanne Kelley works untiringly as managing editor and is now co-director with Alan Davis, who remains senior editor, and Wayne Gudmundson serves as a consultant, now semi-retired and limiting his involvement in the press. Thom Tammaro continues as poetry editor, and Al Sheets remains art director. With students cycling through at annual intervals, New Rivers' community and shared purpose is a constant in the flux of change as New Rivers Press continues to publish fine writing and to teach publishing to students who will one day assume character roles in the ongoing New Rivers Press story.

JOYCE SUTPHEN

Full Stop

Instead of a poem
I draw vortexes, gyring
seashells, tunnels going
in or out, depending.

I play the piano,
slow progressions
almost dissonant but
reaching towards

resolution—perhaps
and depending upon.
I wander through stores
as if racks were
islands, shelves

going fluorescent
like sunless cliffs.
Instead of a poem I
think clouds, what

holds me steady is
not expected,
when I drift and curl
like smoke in air,

circling out from
this first and last stroke
of the pen where I begin
where I end.

DAVID DEFUSCO

David DeFusco is the assistant dean of Strategic Communications at the American University School of Public Affairs. While working on his MFA from Fairfield in Connecticut, he completed a non-resident internship with New Rivers Press.

How to Become a New Rivers Press Author

When I signed up for Fairfield University's master's program in creative writing, my only goal was to attain literary glory. I dreamed of publishing a novel worthy of my heroes—Styron and Steinbeck, for starters—and then hawking it on TV talk shows, at intimate gatherings, at signings for awestruck fans, and in a *New Yorker* interview. And I would use the princely advance to extricate myself from the humdrum of my day job and find a nook somewhere out of earshot of society's bedlam and luxuriate in the writing of the sequel. In my reverie, I'm probably in good company.

But after attending a seminar on the business of writing as part of my master's program, it became clear that I would have to master the less glamorous process of getting published as much as I would the craft of writing. So this guide, or primer, of sorts, is akin to the advice you probably got once from a college career counselor before you went on your very first job interview: To wit, first impressions are critical. The skills you acquired in your MFA program or have mastered on your own are indispensable to achieving your literary ambitions. And you'd be wise to remember the advice your mother or a teacher probably gave you when you were young: Follow the rules.

I interviewed a handful of editors at small or independently owned presses and gleaned information from their websites, since many, if not most, of you will be dealing with them as you embark on your career.

New Rivers Press, according to its website (www.newriverspress. com), was founded in 1968 by C.W. "Bill" Truesdale and has published more than 330 titles. After Truesdale's death in 2001, Alan Davis and Wayne Gudmundson revived and relocated it to Minnesota

State University Moorhead, where its dual mission is to publish literary work of every character, with an emphasis on new and emerging writers, and to provide learning opportunities, including a certificate in publishing, for students in partnership with MSUM. The press honors Truesdale's progressive spirit by publishing work with a strong sense of place that speaks to society's troubled times with *satyagraha* (the truth force), empathy, and aesthetic courage.

New Rivers Press publishes a biennial anthology called *American Fiction*, a series that searches out the best unpublished stories by emerging writers through an open competition. It was twice chosen by *Writers' Digest* as one of the best places in the United States to publish fiction, and contest winners and finalists are distributed nationally by Consortium. Previous judges include Charles Baxter, Ann Beattie, Robert Boswell, Ray Carver, Louise Erdrich, Clint McCown, Antonya Nelson, Joyce Carol Oates, Tim O'Brien, Wallace Stegner, Anne Tyler, and Tobias Wolff.

If you want your short story collection, memoir, novel, or poetry published by New Rivers Press, one of the first things you should do is visit its website. Every press has its own personality, according to managing editor Suzanne Kelley, so it's a good idea for writers to read through websites to determine the right match for you. She recommends that you don't call presses for information that is already present on websites, since staffers at small presses are typically few and hard-pressed for time.

As a teaching press, New Rivers Press authors and students collaborate during the editing process, while Kelley guides and facilitates their efforts. It would be much faster to edit and market the manuscripts herself than to teach others to be analytical and creative in their efforts, but the press's goal is to offer a broad range of experiential learning in the field of publishing to its students.

In addition to MSUM's Master of Fine Arts in Creative Writing program, graduate and undergraduate students interested in learning about the business of publishing can enroll in a practicum in publishing, part of the university's Certificate in Publishing. Alan Davis, professor of English and senior editor at New Rivers Press, oversees screening manuscripts for the Many Voices Project contest, while Kelley assists student teams as they edit manuscripts. The experience is unique among universities and literary presses and prepares students for additional internships or careers in the publishing industry.

When you've determined what press is right for you, you'll need to write a query letter. Every small press I talked to emphasized its importance. It may be more important than all of your lush prose or elegant verse in getting published. The letter should be only a page long and contain a succinct and compelling summary—no more than a paragraph or two—of your book's theme, and also include where you've been published and a few bulleted items that explain how you're going to market your own book—on your dime. Kelley said she would want to see how you plan to reach out to regional bookstores and where you plan to give readings. Make sure you include the obvious details in the letter—your name and contact information—and feel free to e-mail it.

If Davis is intrigued by your letter, you will be asked to submit one to three chapters from your novel or memoir, or five to six samples of poetry. Don't submit your entire collection or book until you're asked. Make sure to include a table of contents so that the acquisitions editor can get a sense of the entire work. If Davis is impressed with the writing or its direction, he will request the entire manuscript and give it a thorough review.

Kelley said it's reasonable to wait three weeks before you contact New Rivers Press about the status of your query letter. You can either call or send an e-mail inquiring as to whether your letter has been received and when you can expect to hear from them. She advises that you not ask whether the manuscript has been read or liked.

New Rivers Press discourages general submissions from November to April so that its staff can pay full attention to its Many Voices Project, an annual competition since 1981 to find new and emerging writers. According to the New Rivers Press terms, an emerging writer has not published more than two books of creative writing with a commercial, university, or national small press. The preferred time for submitting at-large manuscripts is in May, and you can expect an acknowledgement within three weeks. New Rivers Press receives approximately one thousand submissions annually, six hundred of them earmarked for its Many Voices Project competition. The *American Fiction* series usually gets more than four hundred submissions, which are whittled down to twenty or so finalists.

If you win the Many Voices Project competition, you will receive $1,000 and free copies and national distribution through Consortium Book Sales and Distribution. Consortium delivers in time for readings, and New Rivers mails publication announcement cards to journals, associations, festivals, and other venues to bring attention to your book. New Rivers is also active in social networking with a vibrant Facebook page used for promotion and marketing, and they send press releases with copies of each book to reviewers. In addition, you'll be invited to do a reading at the book's launch, and staff will provide you with material for your own advertising and with advice on how to do a reading. Kelley said it's up to you to identify other authors who are familiar with your work for testimonials, or blurbs, that appear on the book's jacket, but that New Rivers Press will help on occasion to obtain them for you.

Kelley said the press has been "getting its toes wet" in electronic publishing, and the press is seeking grants to get its backlist online. The press is aiming to turn all of its prose books into electronic versions, but Kelley said it'll be an expensive proposition if the press seeks to maintain the decades-old philosophy of making its books available to anyone who wants to read them. Besides cost, she said, poetry presents limitations because it "doesn't fit well" in the e-publishing format.

If your work has passed muster with the editors, you'll be offered a contract. What should you expect? The contract should say if you will be paid in advance, how long it will take for the book to be published, and what the publisher will do to drum up sales, even if the language is as simple as "our marketing executive will be taking over your book." Advances and royalties aren't always offered to authors, but if they are, they should be spelled out in the contract.

If you're under contract with New Rivers Press, your primary responsibility is to get your manuscript in to the editor by the contractually specified deadline. The press does not ordinarily give you an advance, but it will begin paying royalties if sales exceed 1,200 copies.

Finally, first-time authors who may have spent years obsessing over their work need to realize that the press ultimately has final say over editorial decisions. Kelley said they're willing to work with you on contested wording or phrasing, but at a certain point you might be told gently, "Let it go."

Unless your book is about vampires or young wizards, chances are you'll be working with a small press. The advantages are legion. Whether it be an established press, like New Rivers, or a fledgling one that's fueled mainly by passion, your manuscript will be given thorough and thoughtful consideration, which is rare at large, for-profit presses. While acquisitions departments in publishing houses of all sizes must consider the profitability of a manuscript, small, not-for-profit presses adhere to the philosophy that there are books that should be read.

From acquisition to final design, small presses also invest an immense amount of resources in the production of a manuscript that might otherwise be considered too expensive by larger presses. Because of their size, small presses tend to be less bureaucratic and more humanistic—qualities that the larger culture should emulate if we are to consider ourselves civilized—so there is more opportunity for you to get to know the entire staff. They represent the best opportunity for a talented, new author to break into the book publishing business. And lest we forget, they produce best-selling titles, too.

Suzzanne Kelley of New Rivers Press put it this way: "If a book starts a conversation among people, then we've filled a void." *A conversation.* Imagine that. Who would have thought that encouraging conversation would someday be considered a niche in publishing? But in an era where people burrow themselves in electronic devices, conversation is exactly what we need to preserve and endow our culture, and small presses, like New Rivers Press, have become dispensaries of truth.

Nick Healy's first collection of short stories was selected as our 125th Many Voices Project award winner for prose. His collection, It Takes You Over, *went on to become a finalist for the Minnesota Book Awards and the Midwest Independent Book Publishers Award, and it won second prize in the Friends of American Writers Award.*

Exuberance or Relief?
A Writer Reflects on the MVP Today
and Awards of All Kinds

*I*f you grow up in St. Paul, Minnesota, as I did, and you are at all interested in writing and literature, you will hear someday the story of when F. Scott Fitzgerald received notice that his first novel had been accepted for publication. He dashed to the street in front of his family's Summit Avenue home, you will be told, and he waved a letter from Maxwell Perkins. He stopped passing motorists and shouted his good news. You will imagine him young and brilliant and exuberant, and the mere thought of him with that letter will bring you joy.

More than twenty years have passed since I first heard the Fitzgerald story. It still makes me smile, and when I thought of it the day New Rivers Press accepted my first book, I had to shake my head and laugh. The call came when I was home with the flu, too sick to read or even to watch television. I'd been asleep when the phone rang, and I would've let it roll into voicemail if I hadn't seen some fragment of "New Rivers Press" on the caller ID. (I'd already been informed that my manuscript was a finalist for the Many Voices Project prize, but I wasn't on pins and needles. When you're a short-story writer you have to learn not to think about the stories you've mailed off to magazines and the manuscripts you've submitted to contests.)

I remember few details of my conversation with Suzanne Kelley, the managing editor and co-director of the press. I'm afraid I sounded like someone in the middle of a fever dream. When we said goodbye and hung up, I stood in my kitchen and stared at a scrap of paper on which I'd noted some crucial details—the release date of my book, something about the prize money, and not much else. I'd imagined this moment before, but I hadn't expected anything like this. I was foggy and feverish, and what I felt was relief, not exuberance.

I'd been sending out various versions of my story collection for a few years, and while it had been short-listed for several national contests, its stars hadn't aligned. Some of those close calls were heartening and heartbreaking at the same time. Just months before New Rivers called, I'd received a letter from the University of Georgia Press informing me that my collection had been a finalist for the Flannery O'Connor Award for Short Fiction but hadn't been a winner. The judge's comments included a particularly memorable line: "This one came close." It was bad news, the best kind of bad news.

This route to publication—through a contest—had seemed odd to me at first, but the simplicity and purity of it held some appeal. I liked the idea of anonymous judging, where every manuscript arrived with an equal chance, regardless of where the writer studied, where she lived, whom he knew, whether she had an agent, or how charming he was at a party. But writers also know that even a contest designed to let merit be its only guide will include some amount of chance. So much depends on the first-round readers, on surviving as a dozen or two manuscripts emerge from hundreds of entries.

After the close calls and consolations, I felt relieved partly because I would finally have an editor and could at last move beyond the mostly solitary days of writing and submitting. In my few notes from the phone conversation with Suzzanne, I had written the phrase "book team," and I knew that soon I'd be hearing from some people assigned to my manuscript. In keeping with New Rivers' mission as a teaching press, the team of students would work under the managing editor. I liked the notion of collaborating with a group of editors, and I'd looked forward to the luxury of a careful, detailed, hands-on edit.

A graduate student named Emily Enger led the book team. She organized the feedback, sent me comments and questions by e-mail, and kept everything moving on schedule. We put some work toward getting the stories into an ideal order, trying to provide a path through the book that would have some rhythm and would pull readers along. The book team asked for only one significant revision, a rewrite of the opening paragraphs to a story called "Lives of Great Northerners." I felt a tug of resistance when I first saw the note. That one had been a rarity—a story published by the first literary magazine I'd sent it to. I'd considered it settled business, but after having some time to think, I took another shot at those paragraphs. The book team had been right. The new version was better.

Soon after the release of *It Takes You Over*, the *Minneapolis Star Tribune* ran a kind and generous review by Anthony Bukoski, which seemed to kick things into gear for me. The next two or three months involved a steady amount of anxiety, but they were also more fun than I'd imagined. And I was back into the world of contests, as New Rivers submitted the book for the Minnesota Book Awards, the Midwest Book Awards, and other prizes.

It might be tempting to dismiss these things—writers do love to give each awards, after all, and there's a bumper crop of award-winning writers still clawing to get their next thing published—but I have to admit it felt pretty good when I heard my book was a finalist for a Minnesota Book Award. I was in my car when I got the news, having just pulled into a parking spot outside a grocery store. I checked my phone for messages and saw a congratulatory e-mail from a friend, who included a link to a list of finalists. There was *It Takes You Over*, right next to Louise Erdrich's *The Round House*, the reigning National Book Award winner. I laughed. There would be no beating her book, but that knowledge didn't diminish my sense of relief.

Relief again? Why? Why not delight or gratification or exuberance? Because if you're like a lot of writers, you live with a fear—or a knowledge—that it might never happen. Even when your latest story gets taken by a magazine you admire, you know that your next story will have to slug its way in somewhere else and that your position in the literary world is hardly less tenuous than it was before you opened the acceptance message. Maybe that's why the Fitzgerald anecdote pleases you so much—because his happiness was pure, because for a moment it didn't matter what came next.

Shortly after the Minnesota Book Awards, where Louise Erdrich gave a fine acceptance speech, I traveled to Chicago for a luncheon hosted by the Friends of American Writers. Each year the group gives prizes to books by Midwestern authors or about the Midwest. *It Takes You Over* had been selected for a 2012 prize, along with two novels published by major houses. The authors were asked to do short readings and to speak about the creation of their book and its path to publication. I thought back to my days of tracking contest deadlines, burning through toner as I printed manuscripts, and hustling down to the post office before closing time. I thought about the scores of writers whose first books have gone into the world with the New Rivers Press logo printed on their spines. It felt good to be part of that tradition. It was an honor and, obviously, a relief.

ELIZABETH SEARLE

Elizabeth Searle is the author of four books of fiction, including Girl Held in Home, *published by New Rivers Press in 2010. Her book* Celebrities in Disgrace *was produced as a short film,* A Four-Sided Bed *is now in development as a feature film, and* Tonya & Nancy: The Rock Opera *has been widely performed, with new productions in the works.*

Reality Fiction and Reality Publishing

*T*he first time a story of mine was selected for a real awards anthology—as opposed to the pretend "collected writings" books I created as a kid, with titles like "Blood & Lipstick"—it was in a volume of New Rivers Press's *American Fiction*, published in 1994.

I was thrilled that the anthology, edited by Al Davis and Michael C. White, deemed me and my fellow contributors to be emerging writers of note. I had just won the Iowa Short Fiction Prize for my first collection. I felt I was "emerging" indeed, and who knew where these early publications might lead?

As is often the case in literary fiction writing, my work and I have traveled a long and winding road since then—one path of which wound up leading me back to New Rivers. I find in the literary life it's good, and realistic, to take the long view.

My relationship with New Rivers Press is a case in point. It began as a first stepping stone in my early career. I renewed my connection with the press years later when I met Al Davis while he and I were both teaching together in Maine. I had followed from afar the inspiring story of how Al and others had helped save New Rivers Press when it was threatened with extinction by joining forces with Minnesota State University Moorhead and successfully transitioning the press into a teaching press where student interns could learn the publishing trade hands-on, working for New Rivers.

By the time I met Al in person, I'd had three books published by fine small presses and I knew it took real grit for a literary press to survive forty-plus years, as New Rivers has done. Years after choosing my fledgling fiction for his anthology, Al still liked my work.

He invited me to give a guest lecture at Minnesota State University Moorhead, where he and the New Rivers crew showed me a good time. The Fargo Film Festival happened to be going on and I recall driving into Fargo with Al to watch the iconic film *Fargo* screened outdoors amidst a blizzard. Al, I knew then, was not only a canny and talented writer and editor, but he was someone with the rare gift of finding artistic and intellectual stimulation wherever he goes. I left my lecture visit with a warm feeling for the cold windswept region where New Rivers Press has managed to take root and flourish.

Fast-forward to 2008. A couple years had passed since my initial New Rivers visit and my writing life had taken an exciting and surprising turn into theater writing. I'd found myself absorbed in creating an opera and a rock opera based on the Tonya Harding/Nancy Kerrigan ice skating scandal. These crazy projects drew crazed amounts of media and drew me away from fiction writing for several years. I'd found the rhythm of writing song lyrics better suited my hectic life as a mother of a lively young son.

Another development in my years away from fiction writing was that, as my husband put it, "people stopped reading." This, anyway, was how it felt when I ventured back into the book-publishing world with my novel *MSS* in the autumn of 2008. I had asked my agent years before if she could see any "crumb" of good news in the flattening out fiction landscape. She'd replied that the only fiction that seemed to gain any attention lately in a book world ruled by nonfiction was fiction connected in some way to a real event.

It so happened that a real and criminal event had taken place in my own neighborhood and that I'd already found myself obsessing on it. I wrote *Girl Held in Home* as a sort of literary thriller—and I was thrilled indeed to get an early blurb from superstar author Tom Perrotta, whose *Little Children* had inspired me in my *Girl* tale and who kindly read my manuscript before we'd even sent it out.

His blurb in turn fired up my agent. As a longtime literary fiction author, I'd always been cautious in my hopes. But with the media I'd drawn for my theater works fueling my confidence, I allowed myself to believe anything was possible when my agent declared my novel ready to send out in early September of 2008.

Then the world economy crashed. One of the tinier casualties of this calamity was the already-reeling publishing industry. When the dust of the 2008 crash settled, while some major New York houses had vanished, smart small presses like New Rivers were still standing—and even, literary rumors had it, thriving in the new world order, which at that time was not much "order" at all, with e-books, self-publishing and beyond all churning up the mix. But I have always liked to stir things up myself.

By 2010, I had a new agent and a new resolve to find a literary press that would be willing to take on a novel with elements of a thriller and work with me to push it in new and different ways. When my can-do new agent heard of my connections at can-do New Rivers Press, he was happy to submit my novel manuscript.

A little background on the book: As noted, *Girl Held in Home* was in fact inspired by a real incident in my neighborhood and it was fueled by my personal experience of being a mom during 9/11 and its aftermath. Here in my home of Arlington, Massachusetts, in 2001, a woman from Indochina was held in a riverfront house as an "unpaid servant" by a family that controlled her visa. I turned the woman into a girl and began to imagine my own story.

My novel's title and its *reality fiction* basis emerged as I wrote my drafts and noticed many news stories centering on young females being held against their will: the so-called "Shed Girl" in California, the "Incest Girl" held in Austria; the famous kidnap victim Elizabeth Smart. In my novel, mixing up all these real elements with my imagination, I told a twisted tale that takes place along the real Mystic River, takes on real post-9/11 issues, and centers on the story of one *Girl Held in Home.*

Yes, the paragraph above owes something to my author's questionnaire, eventually filled out at New Rivers Press. This form—longer and more detailed than any I'd filled out before—was given out to my newly appointed publishing book team at New Rivers, so that they could get to know me and my book from across the miles. All this was explained to me by the gracefully named Suzzanne Kelley, the New Rivers managing editor who, along with Al, had accepted my book and who was spearheading the *Girl Held in Home* team.

A word about that team and about team-work in general at New Rivers and in small-press publishing. I believe it's the spirit of being part of a literary community and supporting work with a focus on getting it out into the world rather than on an often narrow and unrealistic bottom line of profit that has helped presses like New Rivers survive while many New York corporate-run presses have foundered.

From the start, I loved the idea of New Rivers being a "teaching press." One reason I enjoy teaching is that I always find it a privilege to work with young people. To quote Mott the Hoople, "all the young dudes carry the news."

The cover designed for my novel by talented MSUM student Amber Power was a wonderful surprise and is my favorite of all my four book covers. That cover epitomizes to me all the advantages of a press that actually loves literature and takes the time to get to know each book. So many fellow writers I know, while pleased with the money and potential of big presses, have found themselves haplessly hating covers and sometimes changed titles that have no relation to the book they wrote.

In contrast, I feel that Amber's cover for *Girl* imagined a visual for my story beyond any I could have concocted. I love the striking staring single eye, the second eye covered by jaggedly chopped bangs, this image staring at me directly from my own description of the girl in my novel. The lettering font is striking, as if cut from newspaper print by a kidnapper's scissors.

What really makes the cover pop for me is how Amber kept the word *girl* in lowercase lettering while HELD and HOME scream out in headline-style uppercase. I liked that visually even before I realized one reason it works is that it captures in typeface the helplessness of the "girl" being "HELD."

Finally, I love the coloring of the cover: the dark intense inky eye and the subtle mango shade of the skin. Suzzanne Kelley noted the mango connection because a mango plays a role in my plot. With typical thoughtfulness and attention to detail, Suzzanne made sure that at one of our first gatherings promoting the book, an AWP offsite reading in early 2010, she ordered sliced mangos to be served. The mangos complimented the colors on the displayed book jacket, and also held a special meaning for me and others on the team who'd read—really read!—the book.

I wanted to thank Suzzanne personally for that touch and for all her editorial care in going over the galleys, but Suzzanne was stranded in a blizzard in Minnesota while we partied at AWP in DC. I wasn't able to meet Suzzanne or the *Girl* team till I headed to Minnesota for a reading tour in fall of 2010. By then, I had been assigned by Suzzanne my own personal intern. I'd never had one before but as soon as I got my intern at New Rivers, I wished I could hire her for life.

Again, Suzzanne had put extra thought and care into our pairing. Talented and dynamic fiction writer Sarah Z. Sleeper was an MFA student studying with Al Davis at Fairfield MFA, and she brought with her years of experience in journalism, public relations, and more. Smart, funny, super-organized, and beautiful to boot, Sarah was a dream partner for me on the "hustings."

I thoroughly enjoyed my trip to North Dakota and Minnesota and my visit to New Rivers' modest homey office, where lovely and welcoming Suzzanne served me delicious hot soup. I was excited that the New Rivers team managed to snag us radio coverage—where I read from my book and took part in a stirring panel discussion on post-9/11 literature. Another high point was reading at Garrison Keillor's legendary St. Paul bookstore and signing books at Keillor's own desk.

Publicizing any book of fiction these days is an uphill battle. Many fiction books do not get reviewed; I know a number of talented writers from small presses whose books received no reviews at all, so I felt lucky when we nabbed positive reviews from Booklist and several newspapers plus a strong full-page review in *American Book Review*.

Of course every fiction writer these days hopes against hope to nab an award, or some recognition that might hoist their title above the fray. Sarah Sleeper went above and beyond in getting my book entered in every contest we thought worth a shot. She even talked the Pulitzer Prize folks into letting my book in past the deadline. (If I had been lucky enough to be a finalist that year, I would have joined luminaries like Denis Johnson in being snubbed by the inexplicably picky Pulitzer judges.) How I wish I could have lucked out and won an award for Sarah and for New Rivers Press.

Alas, lightning did not strike on the awards front. And of course, life on the book trail was not all roses either. Readings these days are a hit-and-miss game and it's no wonder that young writers I know are eschewing bookstore reading tours for "blog tours" that they can conduct in their pajamas.

But I was of the old school and probably said "yes" to a few too many events. There were stellar gigs well worth doing like a well-paid reading at a beautiful book festival in Virginia. Then there was the night I found myself slogging through Brooklyn in icy rain, trying to locate a tiny bookstore, realizing I was dangerously lost as I passed a godforsaken warehouse building with an ominous sign: LIVE Chickens Slaughtered Here. What, I wondered as I hurried on in sodden terror, am I doing with my life?

Yet somehow I did escape with my life and survive all my book events of frenzied 2011, the same year that my rock opera premiered in Boston. Exhausted by my overdose of onstage activity, I fell ill with pneumonia in 2012, spent a few days in the hospital, and resolved to take things a little slower next time, if I luck into another book tour. But was it worth all the work? To me, yes. I put my heart into my writing and I love having a publisher that puts its heart into the printing and publicizing of the book.

"So how many copies did you sell?" my very practical minded sister asked me well-meaningly after I'd settled back in to work on my next projects.

I told her honestly that I didn't know. While some writers fanatically track their sales figures, however small, I am content to get occasional reports and to take the long view. With my first book, *My Body To You*, published by University of Iowa Press in 1993, it took well over a decade for the original hardback print run to sell out. But sell out it did, eventually, and a beautiful new paperback edition was recently released, giving the book a new life.

As a longtime literary writer, I count my blessings wherever I can and try to keep my hopes realistic. I am pleased whenever I see my books on store shelves and in the library. I was delighted when my hair stylist, not normally a book reader, read *Girl Held in Home* while on jury duty and reported she could not put it down. My niece read it with similar enthusiasm while pregnant and sick in Brazil. Another friendly reader text messaged me that she missed her subway stop reading it. Such are the small rewards along the road in the real world of literary publishing.

Recently a possibility of a new life for my first novel, *A Four-Sided Bed*, has emerged with a small film company developing my own feature-length script of the novel. My script has won some film festival prizes and the project is drawing interest. Similarly, *Girl Held in Home* seems to me and to some theater pros I have recently met to be suited to the stage. With its action-driven plot, much of it taking place in a confined space over a single day, it would be a natural for adaptation. Meanwhile, my interest in the subject of stolen girls continued and I wrote a one-act play inspired by some of the research I did for my *Girl* novel.

Stolen Girl Songs premiered in 2013 at the Northern Writes New Play Festival in Maine and was performed again in late 2013 in the Boston area. With new productions of both my Tonya & Nancy opera and rock opera scheduled for 2014, I am eager to try my script-writing skills on *Girl Held in Home*.

My agent approves my career taking multiple tracks. In today's chaotic publishing world, it makes sense for writers to stay flexible. I admire how New Rivers—while staying true to its roots as a publisher of literary works—also tries its wings in the new world of publishing, working on intriguing multimedia e-books and other adventures.

I will try adapting *Girl Held in Home* as a script and I will keep pushing the novel whenever I can—most recently in a post called "Stolen Girls" for a new woman writers' blog, TheGloriaSirens. And I have incorporated my thoughts on ripped-from-the-headlines fiction like my own *GIRL* in a lecture I've given in various venues on what I call reality fiction.

New Rivers Press is, to me, a fine example of reality publishing. The press is aptly named; it is not one river but many, each winding along in its own way. New Rivers teams up with its authors in facing the realities of the literary landscape today and heads into it suited up as if for a Minnesota winter. Still, the rivers flow. Together, we work our hearts out to get our words out into the real world.

Joe Stracci's debut novel, Whitney, *won the 2012 New Rivers Press Many Voices Project prize for prose. Stracci's essay describes the angst and joy of working with his book team and New Rivers Press.*

A Stupid, Noble Responsibility

I.

*L*ike most writers, I spend a lot of time in my head. Sometimes, it's a great place to be—I know a lot of trivia and obscure facts; I can do decent impersonations; and I can wax poetic on writing and reading, art and music, politics and sociology—a sort of Liberal Arts degree monsoon of Intro To's. And I've always placed value in this kind of approach to life—a rabbinical-esque pursuit of Knowledge.

But other times, quite frankly, my head is a shitty place to be. I get hung up on these . . . let's call them *quests* . . . for the knowledge mentioned above. For example: Before I finally forced myself to sit down and write this essay, I was attempting to compile the original source material for nine Daft Punk samples on their seminal album *Discovery*, spurred on by a YouTube video. But my two streaming music sources, Rdio and Spotify, didn't have all nine of the songs in their catalogs. YouTube only had the original video, but that was only snippets of each song. I then spent some time trying to decide if I should just create one all-encompassing "Dance" playlist, since during the Daft Punk jag, I was also obsessing over Donna Summer's "I Feel Love," since hearing it in *American Hustle* and then hearing it again on KCRW's Guest DJ Project podcast. (The guest DJ was Ru Paul.)

But then I thought to myself: *What if all of the Daft Punk songs aren't necessarily all Dance songs?*

Having dealt with this type of imaginary completist demon before, I forced myself to be OK with only being able to find six of the songs; added the DS song to my "Did You Hear That Song? (2014)" playlist (a place where I keep all the random songs I hear over the course of the year that make me say, well, you can probably guess), and said: *OK, done, time to write.*

But then, a frozen dagger of panic: *What if I want to hear the DS song and then transition right into the Daft Punk playlist? That will require switching back and forth and you know something always goes wrong with that maneuver. And what if I'm doing this while DJ'ing a party? How will that look?*

And on and on and on.

So what the fuck does this all have to do with anything? Especially considering I was told that "the idea [of this essay] is to expose others to what it's like to be a writer, a New Rivers Press award winner, and a published author."

Let's try a different story.

When I started grad school, the urgency to Get Published began ticking inside of me like a time bomb. I'd never much considered it before as a reality, but being around others who did think it a reality (if it wasn't already for them) poked at my competitive nerve. As a sports fan, I quickly came to believe that to Get Published was the equivalent of being called up to The Big Leagues; it meant you'd made it to the pros.

On the final day of my third workshop (I went to Bennington College, a low-residency program; there are four workshops in toto, one every six months), both instructors, David Gates and Tom Bissell, wanted to leave us with a sort of summation, two final bits of advice or thoughts to chew on for the next few months. Tom Bissell told us, and I'm paraphrasing:

Before you've published your first short story, you're going to think: *If only I could publish a story. Everything will be different for me as a writer once I've published a story.*

And then you'll publish your first story, probably in a lower-profile journal or magazine. You'll have that buzz for a day—a real, live, published story!—and then you'll start to think: *If only I could publish a story in a big-time magazine. Everything will be different for me as a writer once I've published a story in a big-time magazine.*

And then you'll publish a story in a big-time magazine. And you'll get the first day buzz again and then you'll start to think: *If only I could sign with an agent. Everything will be different for me as a writer once I sign with an agent.*

And then you'll sign with an agent. You'll get the first day buzz again and then you'll start to think: *If only I could sell my first book. Everything will be different for me as a writer once I sell my first book.*

And then you'll sell your first book. And eventually, if you're lucky, you'll realize that none of those milestones changed you; that you're still the same writer. And the same hard, lonely work that was required to write that first story is still required to write the second or third book. If you're really lucky, you'll even realize that, rather than easier, it might now be harder to continue on maintaining that career of selling books.

II.

Eight hundred words in and I've hardly mentioned New Rivers Press. So let's start with an honest admission: New Rivers Press, the 2011 Many Voices Project, was the end. *Whitney*, my debut novel, had been rejected by more than thirty-seven agents (I stopped counting at thirty-seven) when I finally wrote to Amy Hempel for help. She suggested that I get a copy of *Poets & Writers*, find some suitable contests, and enter the manuscript. I entered three and, since you're reading this, you can probably guess—I won one.

The year-and-a-half long process of turning *Whitney* into an actual book was relatively painless (if not a sobering example of why a Dead Trees-centered Book Publishing Industry, as it exists now, is not a sustainable model)—there were no wholesale rewrites of my words, plenty of my input was taken to heart and acted upon, and I worked with good people who genuinely seemed to care about the process and my book. Each update—a cover, a proof—made the day I received that update the best day of the week, the month. I'll likely be spoiled forever by the experience.

And the size of the press, the informality of much of our interactions, the hands-on spirit that permeated throughout, resonated deeply with my DIY/punk rock roots. As Suzzanne Kelley, New Rivers' managing editor and co-director wrote to me, "As a small press entering its forty-sixth year, we're a bit of a rarity, and to have spent a decade as a teaching press, we are even more unusual." In the age of #LongReads and Content Creation, rarities like New Rivers are a tremendously important counterweight.

But there's another side to that truth.

I'm often nagged by the feeling that I made my way into The Big Leagues via a back door; a technicality. I won a contest, which, colloquially, is almost the same as a sweepstakes. The people that put the wood behind *Whitney*'s arrow are half a country away. Spending time with them for the launch of the book, which I was fortunate enough to do, was surreal—here they were, the people I had only ever e-mailed with, and here I was, intruding on their home turf, as we came together because of our common bond—my words.

And I've told myself many times that in some ways, *Whitney* maybe earned some extra "cred" as a published book by coming to market in the manner that it did—no favors, no I Know Somebody, no connections. It literally rose above the rest of its competition. But, and I'm emotionally raw enough at the moment to write this—I don't really believe that.

Like all artists, I imagined my creation, upon release, being met with stampeding herds, gasped *Oh, my god—have you heard about*s, and librarians protesting calls for bans in the Midwest. And with that, I would finally become A Writer, the last person to walk into the room at readings, the person who, once the crowd of wannabes, up-and-comers, and literary scenesters saw had arrived, made it clear that *this Literary Event can begin now.*

And please, please understand: I hate myself for thinking this. I don't much like literary events, writers—people, for that matter. But it's true. And as a writer, I feel a stupid, noble responsibility to honoring the truth, no matter how messy or unflattering, even if, since *Whitney*'s publication, there have been no herds, no gasps, no librarians, no bans for them to protest.

III.

When I write personal essays, I always start with the assumption that at some point I will use a form of the phrase: *I've got no idea what this all means.* I like beginning with that doubt. It means that the potential (honest) notion that *this is all bullshit* is organically a part of the DNA of the piece.

Like scientific truth, personal victories are few and far between, usually undermined by our insistence on wondering what bigger personal victories can be derived from them. Artists take it a masochistic step further, as they have to fight the realization that every step towards success takes them further away from the painful place that spurred them on. And then there are writers, who "write for themselves" and when they're finished, ask the world: *Want to see what I wrote?*

So here goes—I have no clue if any of this will mean anything one day—*Whitney*, New Rivers Press, my career as a writer, etc. If we're speaking only in terms of probability, then let's be honest—it will probably mean nothing. The world is full, literally, of used books that sell for pennies on the Internet. And in a sad, pessimistic way, at this point, I'd be happy to see used copies of *Whitney* selling for pennies, as it would mean someone bought it in the first place.

As far as I see it, I have two choices: I can tread water in my head for nothing, get nothing out of it. I can make playlists and listen to podcasts and rifle through the mental filing cabinets, looking and feeling busy, filling them with stuff, jotting down my descriptions of the world, impressing the three of four people who see my words, all while chasing the next artistic Choose Your Own Adventure buzz, dreaming about the fortune and fame that awaits me when I finally get my Agent, when I finally step up to the plate in The Big Leagues, wearing the uniform of a Big Publishing House.

Or—

I can think back to the day, July 12, 2012, that Al Davis called me to tell me that Debra Marquart has chosen *Whitney* as the prose winner of the 2011 Many Voices Project. I was sitting at my desk at my 9-5 job, imaging what life would be like once I finally sold my first book. After I hung up, I called my wife at work. When she answered, I simply said, "I won."

I can think back to my trip to Moorhead, Minnesota, to New Rivers Press, glorious time spent in my head; real quality there's-synergy-in-everything-around-me, way-down-the-rabbit-hole type time spent in my head. The cigarettes I smoked while enjoying the perfectly cinematically mundane view outside of my hotel of the highway and the commercial landscape. The people I met. The cold. My broken leather jacket zipper. The blur and buzz of five flights in three days. The readings. The music I listened to. How much sense it all made. Feeling for three days like I'd made it to The Big Leagues.

Want to be a writer?

Learn how to soak all of that in, wring yourself out, and move on—and then get to work on the next thing.

The next thing will change everything.

JOYCE SUTPHEN

Untitled, Hiroshige

Is that a lantern or a
moon in the willows?

And what are those stars
saying to the man in the boat?

Where is there a blue so deep
as the blue between the banks

of the reedy shore? The clouds
are floating. No one here

has ever read the Bible or
watched a tornado touching down.

Dynamic Range

Nancy Swan, who writes of the West and the rugged individuals intimately ingrained in its past, present, and future, came to New Rivers Press as a low-residency intern with the Stonecoast MFA in Creative Writing.

An Internship at New Rivers Press

September 1, 2009. The sun is only two hours up in the eastern sky and already heat radiates off my driveway as I labor under the weight of my luggage. Arizona doesn't know we are heading into fall. Thin-blooded as I am after seventeen years in the sun-drenched desert, I have packed stacks of sweaters, long underwear, heavy corduroy slacks, jeans, jackets, gloves, fuzzy neck wraps, warm caps, a pair of fur-lined boots, and two sets of heavy flannel pajamas for my time in the Midwest. I am nervous, excited, jubilant, and worried about my jubilance. Am I nuts? I'm sixty-three and going to drive almost two thousand miles with a five-foot by eight-foot enclosed utility trailer in tow to a rooming house in Fargo that I found on the Internet. I wipe the sweat from my forehead and heave a box of books that I must have with me, and another box loaded with my dog's food, bowls, bed, and grooming equipment. Rosie, a five-year-old golden Lab, will be taking up the backseat of my truck. She will keep me out of harm's way. She always has.

I go over my checklist: house phone programmed with message to call my cell; air conditioning set on ninety degrees; houseplants farmed out to friends; newspaper stopped; mail forwarded to Fargo rooming house that allows dogs and has a fenced yard; timers on indoor lights set to go on at 7:00 p.m. and off at 10:30 p.m.; boy down the street paid to mow lawn and keep up with weeding; Neighborhood Watch alerted I will be gone; e-mail sent to New Rivers Press announcing my arrival date of September 8. And that's it. I'm ready.

"You and me, Rosie. Here we go." Into the wild blue yonder.

I head up through the northwest corner of New Mexico, planning to stop for two nights in Colorado with friends. The drive is gorgeous, aspens on the mountains shimmering yellow in the cool fall air.

The following two days are the Wyoming crossing, land of Gretel Ehrlich and her fabulous anthology, *Solace of Open Spaces*, a book that speaks to my heart. Ehrlich writes of loss and of her recovery of self in the ranching life in Wyoming. I, too, have found the same healing power in nature throughout my life. Leaning back against a cottonwood tree on our stop for lunch, I read to Rosie from "The Smooth Skull of Winter," my favorite of Ehrlich's stories of Wyoming. We head back to the truck, due east now, headed for Rapid City, South Dakota. Then, finally, on to Fargo, North Dakota.

***

September 8. My first meeting at New Rivers Press, I was late. Fargo has more one-way streets than anywhere I've ever driven before. I got lost along the Red River, which was frustrating as I could see the other side, knew I had to cross to it to get to the university in Moorhead but couldn't seem to quite get it right. Orange cones demarcated work areas on many of the two-way roads, signs sending me on detours to parts unknown. Couldn't seem to quite get that right either. Sweat gathered in my armpits. I'd left my cell phone on the dresser so a quick call wasn't an option. Damn.

Even so, the most fantastic thing happened. When I burst through the office door at Weld Hall where New Rivers Press was housed, everyone smiled at me. Broad, happy smiles. Alan Davis stood to greet me, steering me to an empty chair at the table. I sat down, we did introductions (Director Wayne Gudmundson, Outgoing Managing Editor Donna Carlson, Incoming Managing Editor and Co-Director Suzzanne Kelley, and, of course, Senior Editor and Co-Director Alan Davis), and then they went on with business as usual. The group was discussing a problem they were having with a new author, Susan Barr-Toman, and her upcoming book, *When Love Was Clean Underwear*. This was the author's first book to come to print, and she was overly anxious about the stewardship of her firstborn. I sat at the table and listened to the compassionate discussion of the issues—primarily her need for constant reinforcement as to the production timeline and the flurry of communications she was generating with questions.

Placing a hand on the table and looking over at me, Alan smiled. "Nancy, this would be a good place for you to jump in. Will you take Barr-Toman on and help her through the nuts and bolts of all this? Her book should be out in October, but until then we need a good PR person to take her to the finish line."

I was stunned, felt my eyebrows rise and eyes widen as I opened my mouth and took a breath. "Sure," I breathed out. "Of course. I can do that."

My face is an open book, or so I've been told. Alan's eyes twinkled. "We'll give you any info you need as her questions come up. Just establish a relationship through e-mail, by phone if necessary, and be her contact person."

"You'll need a title," Wayne Gudmundson chimed in. "How about Editorial Assistant? That'll work."

"Right," I said, writing in my notebook. Susan Barr-Toman. *When Love Was Clean Underwear*. OK. Me, Editorial Assistant. I couldn't believe it. I was official!

The discussion turned to the transitions New Rivers was experiencing. It had been a tumultuous spring and summer, complete with an office move, and massive flooding of the Red River, and, moreover, they were undergoing a management change. Long-time manager Donna Carlson was planning to move out of state and Suzzanne Kelley was just now going through her orientation period. It was immediately clear that I could either be a help or a hindrance in the delicate balance of things, and I decided right then to be the very best I could be.

During the meeting, I studied the New Rivers staff. Both men relaxed back in their chairs. Alan was dressed in jeans and a brown pullover sweater. Occasionally his face would light with animation, dark eyes bright behind his glasses. Wayne wore khakis and a beige shirt open at the collar, and his demeanor was more subdued than Alan's but engaging still. Donna looked exhausted and harried, her eyes tired as they peered owl-like from her glasses. She was the most formally dressed in a white silk blouse and long skirt. In contrast, Suzzanne wore cotton pants and a black pullover, the hue setting off the long blond waves of her hair. She had an interesting habit of tilting her head whenever she spoke, arms crossed, one hand raised to cup her chin. I wondered how I looked to them—nervous? Tentative? Confident?

When the meeting was over, I asked for a galley copy of Barr-Toman's book so I could read it that night and feel better prepared to befriend her the next day. Alan pulled one from his briefcase. Suzzanne gave me a hug as I left with book in hand, whispered "Good luck," and gave me a sympathetic smile.

Before leaving the office, I noticed a stack of boxes pushed against the wall. Packages of varying sizes almost overflowed from them.

"Behind on your mail?" I quipped.

"Manuscripts coming in for the Many Voices Project competition. We'll go into that another day," Alan responded. "You might be able to help us out there, too." He smiled an enigmatic smile.

After a tour of the campus with Suzzanne, I headed for my car in high spirits. There on my windshield was a parking ticket from Campus Security. Wrong lot. Oh, well. I had roared into the first open space I saw when I was late. Even the ticket could not dampen my enthusiasm.

Left to right: Suzzanne Kelley, Donna Carlson, Nancy Swan; Open House at New Rivers Press, Minnesota State University Moorhead, 2009. New Rivers Press Archives.

***

September 9. Walking from my car to the office, *When Love Was Clean Underwear* tucked into my leather tote and a large cup of hot coffee in my hand, I reveled in the fall colors adorning the campus. The day looked fine; I felt even finer though I had been up until 3:00 a.m. reading "my" author's book. The sun was shining, the air crisp and clean. No need for the long underwear yet. I was a happy camper. Suzzanne and Donna were in the office already, heads together over Donna's almost-ex desk. They looked a bit harried as their heads rose in unison to greet me.

"Can you get your first e-mail off to B-T (Barr-Toman) this morning? She's asking about her postcards, which haven't been run yet." Donna had a worry-line going on her forehead.

"Postcards?"

Donna gave me the run-through. Each author they published was supplied with a stack of postcards, the book cover on one side of the card and one or two promotional blurbs on the other. The cards were printed with addresses the author supplied to New Rivers as a promotional mailing list. B-T's addresses were still waiting to be converted to an Excel spreadsheet. Donna pointed me to a desk with a computer, gave me B-T's e-mail address and the notes of her latest calls and turned me loose.

"Be sure to let us take a look at whatever you compose before you send it, please," she asked, turning back to her desk and Suzzanne.

"You can be sure," I responded. After all, once I hit "send," the e-mail couldn't be taken back. I set down my coffee and notebook, took off my sweater, fired up the computer, and began to write my first intern-to-author note. I introduced myself and offered the author whatever support she needed as her book came to print. I let her know we were working on preparations for running her postcards and would let her know the moment they were ready for mailing.

Just as I finished the note, Alan walked into the office. "Hey, working already, are you?"

"Will you take a look before I hit 'send'?" I pointed to my computer screen.

He rapidly scanned the text. "Great, great. She'll love this. Thanks. Send it."

And out it went. Twenty minutes later, I had a response. Our correspondence continued: What was the cost to have prepaid postage applied to postcards? (Expensive.) Where exactly was the book in the production process? (Five weeks out to print.) And again, could the postcards be done sooner than later? (Unfortunately, no.) The empathy I felt for B-T's situation, almost identical with that of a new mother calling her pediatrician constantly, helped to form my responses to her issues as she counted down the days. After all, I hoped to be a first-time novelist someday. I got it.

As Alan moved about the office fielding questions posed by Donna and Suzzanne, he also included me in the conversations. "Nancy, you could help out with that."

I took rapid notes in a scrawling hand. Work with Ryan Christiansen on new website—many New Rivers book covers not scanned yet—FIND BOOKS FOR SCANNING.

Alan continued. "Suzzanne, you could take Nancy to the catacombs and show her our back inventory storage area. She could look for the missing books there." He paused a moment. "Nancy could work on the design team, too. Al Sheets—he's the art director for New Rivers Press and works here at the university, Nancy—will be at the next meeting and we'll make introductions then." He turned to me. "You would enjoy the art part of the books, wouldn't you?"

"Absolutely!" My pen moved at one hundred miles per hour. Design Team. Al Sheets. Meeting next week. Yay!

After only two days, I was a part of the group, ready to be overworked and filled with the light that seemed to suffuse the staff in the face of great difficulties. I went to the Rolodex, picked up the phone and called Ryan Christiansen (the young man working on the new website) to set up a date to talk about his project and see what I could do to help.

That night I lay in my bed, Rosie's head on my belly warming me like a hot water bottle. Not that I wasn't warm enough. I was on fire with excitement from the day. I was feeling the eye of the tiger, hungry for the feast before me.

***

September 10-11. The New Rivers office was locked when I arrived, a note from Suzzanne taped to the door saying she and Donna would be in at 2:00 p.m. I climbed the worn carpet-clad stairs to the second floor where Alan had his private office for consults with students and colleagues. The door stood open and I stepped in.

"Hey, Alan! Can I have a key to the office? Suzzanne and Donna are out until this afternoon."

Alan looked up from a text he was studying. "Hey to you, too, Nance. Let's fix you up with a key, and I want to get you a parking pass as well."

"Super. I already got one ticket parking in the wrong place when I was late."

Back downstairs, I proudly opened the office door with my personal key, checked messages on the phone, and wrote notes for Suzzanne. Then I began to go through those books on the shelves in the office, hoping to find a title or two on the "missing" list for book covers for the new website. I was thrilled to find four. I checked my e-mail. There were two messages from B-T. I answered back with empathy for her long wait and reiterated New Rivers' commitment to quality in the production of her book. To move her onto more positive thoughts, I asked about her background and history as a writer and if she was currently working on something new. She responded that she was teaching creative writing at Temple University and currently working on another novel. In closing she apologized for possibly overusing her "e-mail rights" and said she would try to be more patient.

The following day I met with Suzzanne at the Annex. It was a post-war bunker-like building located at one corner of the campus. It had a deep, dark basement filled with metal shelving stacked with books. She educated me briefly on the problems inherent in stocking too many volumes and the storage requirements involved. Ordering books printed on demand was something New Rivers was considering to resolve this issue. Suzzanne asked if I was OK working in what she called the catacombs by myself. I replied "Yes," she patted me on the back, picked up her purse, and left. Although the space was dreary and imposing, I was in heaven, alone and surrounded by books without a thing to disturb my quest. I worked all morning, finding most of the titles that needed scanning, then broke for lunch.

After lunch I went back to my search but found nothing more. Four books remained missing, but I otherwise was on top of my first project. I went back to the office and e-mailed Ryan to let him know I had a stack of books ready. We arranged to meet Monday morning to pass off the books I had accumulated.

***

September 14. I was into the office by 10:00 a.m., planning to work until 5:00 p.m. Suzzanne and I walked to the post office across campus to pick up mail. A huge stack of manuscripts waited there, and we needed a cart to wheel them back across the quad to the office. The Many Voices Project competition was obviously gearing up. Suzzanne made a comment to the effect that the data entry process for the competition would begin soon, and I had a portent of my next project.

After unloading the cart and taking it back to the post office, Suzzanne and I rearranged the furniture in the office. The upcoming open house to show off New Rivers' new digs was on September 30 and we were preparing ahead of schedule. We cleaned the storeroom, giving me a chance to acquaint myself with the location of supplies and the office filing system. I redid the old labels on the bookshelves, delineating books by the year they were published. It seemed to me to be a system that could be improved upon—possibly lining the books up alphabetically by authors' names—but I decided to wait a few weeks to bring that up at a meeting sometime. I didn't want to seem pushy. Tired and bedraggled by 4:30 p.m., we called it a day and closed the office.

***

September 15. The office meeting started punctually at 2:00 p.m. Wayne, Alan, Suzzanne, Donna, and I were present. Al Sheets was in attendance, too, and Alan introduced us. I noted with interest that his clothes were more colorful in nature than those worn by Wayne, Alan, Donna, or Suzzanne. But, then, he was the art director, wasn't he?

We all gathered around the small meeting table. Alan turned the time over to Al and he set up the dates for upcoming gatherings of the design team. The team was comprised in part by Al and several art students, all of whom would be reading books chosen for publication and designing covers and interiors. Alan, Suzzanne, Wayne, and I would also be on the team. It was an exciting project. Alan gave me preview copies of the books to read—there would be four—and I packed them into my leather tote. I could hardly wait to start reading and thinking about designs for covers.

The meeting went on to other topics. The first was the Many Voices Project. Alan explained to me that the MVP had its origin in the desire to promote new and emerging writers as part of the mission statement of New Rivers Press. It is a national writing competition open to both prose (fiction and creative nonfiction) and poetry. A "blind" contest, the authors' identities would be unknown to the judges.

Alan sat forward in his chair. "How are your typing skills, Nancy?"

Since I had been a medical transcriptionist for twenty-eight years, they were excellent, and I said so.

Alan leaned back in his chair, an exaggerated sigh escaping his lips. "Ah, yes. Great! Will you take on the data entry process for the MVP? It's just a spreadsheet of information." His eyes crinkled. "Well, actually a very long, long spreadsheet. Can you help us out?"

I jumped from the frying pan into the fire. "Happy to do it, Alan. Point the way."

Another student working part time for New Rivers would show me how to set up the spreadsheet and get me started. I scrawled notes in my notebook. Call Sammi and set up appointment to learn about data entry process for MVP.

"And since you're working with B-T, can you handle some correspondence with Elizabeth Oness? We just published her book, *Fallibility*, and she has some requests piled up regarding promotional material for readings she wants to set up. Shouldn't take too long to deal with, but we just haven't had the time what with the move and the transition from Donna to Suzzanne."

"Sure. In fact, I just read her book this weekend. Took it off the shelf when I was searching books for Ryan. It's beautiful poetry. I'll e-mail her right away." Note: Contact Oness. Get addresses of reading venues and send out PR letters reiterating quality of book. I left the meeting with a full plate—the days ahead would be crammed with work, just the way I wanted it.

***

September 16. I learned that Nick Flynn, author of *Another Bullshit Night in Suck City*, was coming to the campus to speak under the auspices of New Rivers Press. I was enervated by the prospect of meeting him and hearing his lecture on writing motivations. Once more, the abundance of this experience at the press almost overwhelmed me and

I was filled with gratitude for the opportunities to learn that just kept coming. A feast, in my book.

I met with Sammi and began the data entry process on the MVP competition. As I unwrapped the first manuscript, I was struck by the care with which it was packaged: layers and layers of packing tape then postal paper, beneath that a box stuffed with Styrofoam bubbles so the manuscript wouldn't jiggle in its container. These budding writers cherished their art and feared the vagaries of the postal system. As a writer myself, I got it. I resolved to give each delivery the care it deserved and went to work in a sea of writing.

***

September 17. I was up early and into the office at 9:00 a.m. ready to rock on my major project. Alan came in right behind me pushing another postal trolley stacked with manuscript packages. His eyes were bright, cheeks flushed, and he looked as happy as a boy with his first BB gun.

"Look at this, will you?"

I was looking . . . at my work for the next month and a half. He could hardly push the trolley it was so loaded down.

"Fantastic." Alan rubbed his hands together, slapped one against the metal handle on the pushcart. "We're in business, Nancy, this is what the MVP is about—all these new artists vying for a place, wanting to be heard. And it's money in the bank for NRP!"

"How many manuscripts are you anticipating, Alan?"

"Maybe five hundred. I'm hoping for that anyway. They'll really start pouring in soon. The deadline for entries is coming up."

Holy shit. Five hundred of these packages to open and process.

"Wow." I exhaled. "Pretty exciting." My fingers itched to get started. There was a long journey ahead. I turned on my computer, brought up the spreadsheet for the application process, found a pair of scissors in a drawer, and got to work.

Alan put a hand on my shoulder. "Is it too much for you? If it is, just say so and we can put Sammi on part of it."

"I can get it done. I'm almost finished with the website work for Ryan, and the PR work with B-T and Oness is going fine, so I'm in good shape. Oh, and the design team readings. I'll need some time to make that happen, but not a problem." For some strange reason, I actually wanted to accomplish the MVP task all on my own, leave something behind after I had gone back to Arizona, something big.

That first day I finished only six entries. There were interruptions as in any office: discussions of ongoing work, phones to answer when Suzzanne was busy, talkative students to converse with as they dropped into the office looking for Alan or information on the publishing class or whatever. Even so, there was a knee-high pile of boxes, bubble wrap, twisted-up tape, and postal paper swarming the floor around my desk. One contestant had used a box that could have accommodated three footballs, then stuffed it with newspaper so his manuscript wouldn't budge an inch. I had given up using the little wastebaskets when I opened that box and decided that I needed a major receptacle. Before leaving the office for the day I located the janitor, told him what was going on in the office and that I needed help—one of the large waste cans on wheels that I could bring to the office every day when I was working on my project. He happily provided one, promising it would be outside the janitorial area every morning. I left the office feeling a little bit more in control, if only of the trash problem.

***

The week of September 21 began my work in earnest at New Rivers. I had a hefty project to complete, and I was determined to do an excellent job. Day after day I slogged through packages—cutting my way through tape, slicing open Priority Mail envelopes, prying into boxes, crumpling bubble wrap and newspaper and tossing them into my giant trash bin. Then the detail work of perusing the entry forms and checks for signatures, removing any pages in manuscripts that could identify the authorship to the judges, cataloguing and coding each manuscript for the readers, and completing the data entry process. I grew fast and efficient at my task, getting it down to approximately twenty minutes per entry. I was never bored, never frustrated, sometimes fatigued, and always filled with purpose. Lines of writing flashed before my eyes, titles caught my imagination or caused me to grimace, even addresses of writers captivated me. One in particular gave me a grin, a manuscript from Mechanicsville, Pennsylvania. How ironic an origin for a literary manuscript, I thought, and it stayed with me.

As I worked on the MVP competition, I answered phones for Suzzanne when she was busy or out of the office, dealt with B-T's questions (May I please have extra postcards when they're printed?), and handled the occasional PR mailing for Elizabeth Oness regarding her proposed readings of *Fallibility*. I ran errands (primarily to the post office and back collecting manuscripts). Ryan Christiansen and I had completed the scanning of book covers for the new website. I attended an art history lecture with Suzzanne, and dined out with newfound friends from campus. It was a stimulating time in my life, swept up in a whirlwind of activities that satisfied the artist within.

Interspersed with all of this was the design team project. Although I was a minor player, the concept enchanted me—read a book, then form a mental picture of the cover design. We would be working on four books, both prose and poetry. This meant many hours of delightful reading ahead but a tight schedule. Every night I set aside time for this activity, took notes, and envisioned book covers.

One day while working in the office by myself, the phone rang. I answered "New Rivers Press. Nancy speaking." The voice on the other end of the line said, "This is Richard Hoffman calling. Is Donna there?"

"Richard, it's Nancy Swan from Stonecoast," I burst out. I knew we were in the process of publishing his book of short stories, *Interference*, but I had not had any opportunity to work on that project yet. We knew one another from the Stonecoast MFA Writers' Program at the University of Southern Maine where I was enrolled as a low-residency student; he was a respected teacher and mentor.

Richard was tickled to find me at New Rivers and asked what I was doing there. My enthusiasm gushed into the phone as I related my activities to him. After a couple of minutes, I regrouped and told him that Donna had been replaced by Suzzanne, that Suzzanne was out of the office, and I was manning the phones. I asked what I could do for him.

"Well," he began, "I'm calling with some changes I want made before *Interference* goes to print. Can you handle this for me?" We spent twenty minutes going over his material. I could feel tension in his voice. "Nancy, I've got a major reading set up for the end of October. Do you know exactly when the book will be out?"

So even Richard, a seasoned veteran with three books under his belt, was experiencing the end-of-cycle tremors that B-T was going through.

"I'll pass these changes on, Richard. If Alan agrees, I'll work on the galley myself. And I'm sure we're on target with your deadline, but I'll reconfirm to you tomorrow. Will that work?" I carefully wrote down his phone number and underscored it three times. HANDLE TODAY, I added.

That afternoon I found Alan in his office and relayed the conversation with Richard. Alan pulled a galley copy of *Interference* from a stack of paperwork on his desk and handed it to me.

"Can you make those changes on here and get it to Suzzanne by tomorrow morning? And, if you have time, do a quick run-through to see if you spot any errors we've missed. And call Richard and tell him we're on schedule for the printing." Alan cleaned his glasses with the corner of his sweater, rubbed his face with one hand. "He's put a lot of work into organizing this reading, I know. It all comes together at once in this business, Nancy." He paused a moment, put his glasses back on. "How's Barr-Toman doing? Is she holding up?"

"She's doing great, Alan, hanging in there like a pro." I thought of her notes, some arriving in my e-mail as late as 11:00 at night. "We're doing fine."

That night I sat at my desk making notations on the galley Alan had given me and thinking once again about the stresses of publishing and being published. It was an enlightening experience getting a look at both sides of the coin.

***

The time flew by. Before I knew it, my months with New Rivers were drawing to a close. Susan Barr-Toman's book came out on schedule. Richard Hoffman's book came out on schedule. Nick Flynn's lecture on campus was a resounding success. I was able to see two book covers come to fruition with the design team. Two were still in process as I prepared to head back to Arizona. The MVP data entry project was complete, and I felt I had contributed something meaningful to the contest. I dropped an e-mail to Elizabeth Oness and Susan Barr-Toman letting them know that I was leaving but that Suzzanne would see to anything else they needed.

With a heavy heart, I packed my belongings at the boarding house. I vacuumed thoroughly to get up Rosie's dust bunnies. I polished the furniture and cleaned the windows.

On November 3, I set out for Arizona, back through South Dakota, Wyoming, Colorado, then New Mexico. As I drove, I thought of the amazing experiences I had at New Rivers and all that I had learned. On November 7, I arrived home. I threw open the windows of my house—it was still lovely fall weather in Arizona—watched Rosie gallop around checking out every corner, announcing her arrival to all the dogs on the adjoining properties. I changed the message on my phone back to the original. Having called ahead to stop the forwarding on my mail, I walked out to the mailbox to collect what had come in. It took all of a day to put things back in order in my home.

It was a bit of a time warp from New Rivers to Camp Verde, Arizona, all of a sudden and in record time. I poured a glass of tea and took it out on the patio, needing a quiet moment to regroup. I was already missing my companions at the office, missing the charged atmosphere of academia and publishing. But I knew my internship experience would live on with me as I labored at my writing, in unexpected moments as I walked Rosie, and in my heart, always. I thought of my mentor and friend, Alan Davis, who had made this possible for me. And I began to plan my Stonecoast third semester project, a paper titled "An Internship at New Rivers Press."

JOYCE SUTPHEN

Apostrophe

This is how we begin—
speaking easy

letting the words
slide down the margin

space in between the stanzas,
breath pulled into lines

of ink, our fingers tapping
to the lift of long riffs

of meter, of now, time's
signature, the future

key of flesh, key of bone,
ad-libbing as we go

no matter how
(or when) it ends.

DANIEL SHUDLICK

Daniel Shudlick is a recent graduate of the Minnesota State University Moorhead MFA for Creative Writing program. He interned at New Rivers Press for more than three years, learning how to market and publicize the press and how to design book covers and interiors.

A Beginner's Guide to Designing
an Interior, By a Beginner

I set the six books down in front of my parents. My mom immediately opened *The Way of All Flux* to the ISBN page and looked for my name. She pointed it out with a little laugh then continued paging through the collection of poems. Her eye for detail noticed the differing fonts from title to poem immediately. "I like that you did it this way," she said. My dad held the books in his hands, each one in their own turn, then set them down and picked up another. For each, he read the titles, opened to the middle of the book, and read a page or a poem. He touched the inside of them with one stroke along the seam. I wondered if he hadn't opened a book but for law reviews and documents for some time. I remember going with him when I was a child to his office in the evenings, him sitting back in his chair reading page after page, while I wandered through the office looking at the pictures on the wall or the Internet, or reading a book of my own. He looked the same, yet entirely different, paging through the books, taking his time with the words.

I talked with my mother about how I lined up the photos in *American Fiction Volume 12*, and also what I would like to do with them if given a second go around. They have traveled six hours to Fargo, and this was what I gave them, books. There's something to the printed book, however—whether its texture, its place on a shelf, in one's hands, stacked together on a coffee table; or in reading a book and a sense of moving forward, the page turn, line to line, word to word, each distinctly placed—that has the power to ensnare the imagination and takes us to different worlds.

So, I sat back and let them have their look. Dad finally set them down. "You did this?"

"No, just the interiors," Mom returned.

He looked through the books again, picking one up, paging through it, setting it down. "How was it?" he asked. "How was it designing the interior?"

At first I just looked at the books. *Where to begin? With the words, yes, with the words.*

"First," I said, "I read the manuscripts." But as I look back on it, that wasn't entirely true.

***

I was not sure what to expect first walking into New Rivers Press, but excitement and wonder filled me nonetheless. I met Dr. Suzzanne Kelley, managing editor at New Rivers Press, right when I walked in the door. Her light and easygoing energy validated my excitement. We sat down and she asked what I was hoping to do at the press, as well as my work history. I told her I was up for pretty much anything. I'd had experience working in an office doing administrative duties, so I figured I would be able to help that way if not in another manner.

"How about interior design?" she asked.

"I haven't done that, but that'd be pretty awesome." I cannot recall exactly what I said, awesome, sweet, cool, or fantastic, but it was something along those lines. I was intrigued and hooked. She then explained what interior design meant, who to meet and talk to for help with the projects, and spoke about some of the editorial language that has become part of the everyday vernacular. At that time, though, I was a bit blown away. My excitement quickly turned to nervousness similar to being in water just a bit too deep, straining to stay above the surface.

"It won't only be on you," she said. And, boy, she was right. Throughout the process, Suzanne helped out, reviewed, and instructed when necessary. Yet, she allowed me to make my own mistakes and find my own answers. To her I am incredibly thankful for her patience as well as determination, but that is getting too far ahead.

Under the new role of interior designer, I began by reading the InDesign CS5.5 handbook (now completely outdated). I took it home with me and read the relevant parts. I had never worked with InDesign before; most templates I used and designed were within Word, Excel, or other Office programs. So, the first time I tried to put text into InDesign, I tried to cut and paste from a Word document. It didn't work well. I could get into the details about what happened, but that may invoke a minor case of anxiety that I'd be wise just to let be. Next, I tried to "Bridge" the document. This was an utter failure and completely disregarded what Bridge within In-Design is meant for, but I tried anyway.

Later that weekend, while paging through the handbook, I came across Place. Place allows text, picture, hyperlink, etc. to be loaded into a preset location within the InDesign document. I was ecstatic. I went back the next Monday and clicked File, Place, selected the document, and there I had it. So I thought. When the document went into the InDesign program, InDesign displayed only the first page of the twenty-five-page document. At the bottom right of the text box glared a red plus sign, which means the entirety of the text cannot fit into the text frame. I clicked on it and found that I could link pages together, so I began to do that. I added new pages and slowly linked one page to the next. However, the text got all jumbled up and I had to move pages around and reformat line by line. It took me two hours to put the twenty-five pages in the right order. I remember the feeling after doing so: complete and unequivocal satisfaction.

In revisiting the manual later that night, I saw the auto-flow section of Place. In my excitement of finding how to place a document, I missed this crucial detail. The auto-flow option allows a document to be placed, in its entirety, one page after another without having to manually link the pages. All it took was holding down the shift button when I placed the text into the InDesign document. It took all of three seconds.

All was not lost. Because of my earlier folly, I learned how to link text to text, text to pictures, etc. Linking pages and bridging are useful for newsletter columns, newspapers or any other medium where one part is connected to another with other text and photos in between (think headline article continued on a back page of a local paper, or where revisions or text of one section need to be the same in another). Although linking stories is not needed, except for a table of contents page (which is a whole other issue), it's nice to know how to link pages from hands-on experience, even if the experience was a complete mistake.

After finally placing the text, I began to manipulate the paragraph formations, the character styles, and different fonts, seeing how they read, effects of size difference and readability, how many characters per line, how many lines per page, etc; margin width; master page applications; and many other forms. As I did this I still had no idea how to construct a readable piece of art, a book from a manuscript. To figure this out, I read online articles, looked at different studies and discussed psychology of reading with colleagues, friends, and family. All this was well and good, but I still felt at a loss within the book design element. After a discussion with Suzzanne, I sent an e-mail to Allen Sheets, professor of graphic design and art director for the press, to see if he would give me a few pointers to lead me in the process.

Although we met only once, Sheets gave me enough information in that one meeting to carry me through the entire process. He suggested books on typography, gave definitive margin widths, alluded to leading standards within font sizes, suggested kerning features for widows and orphans, suggested font-types, and told me where to look for additional information. Much of my understanding about the history of interior design, typography, and type-setting, has a great deal to do with that conversation and a few e-mails following it, for if the knowledge I have did not stem from that exact conversation, it has stemmed from ideas and research starting points that we discussed.

A few weeks later, Suzzanne gave me the manuscripts to read. The first was *Haints* by Clint McCown. The story circumnavigates a quiet southern town struck by a tornado in in the early '50s. One of the motifs within the novel is that of ghosts—individual, familial, cultural. With this narrative, also taking a look at the type from the book cover, I wanted a more haunting font. The text, particularly the chapter headings, I thought should have a bit more flair or more of a script-like feel to it. The script of the chapter headings text is based, but not exactly, on the design of the "H" in *Haints* on the cover. This idea was taken from some advice I received from Dr. Thom Tammaro, poet, English instructor, and MFA director at MSUM, to repeat a small thread throughout the design of the novel. It is small, but the eyes manage to make the transition from the cover to the first page with ease and comfort.

I used more of a trial and error approach in choosing the font for the main text, in gaining a sense of the piece as it looks on the page. Even though I researched different fonts and font families, the single line or paragraph given in the examples did not always translate, visually, into a large body of text. I had liked a few fonts when in a single line, but when I applied the font to the larger text, they looked clunky or did not work. Sometimes the font spacing was too far apart or too crunched, making it difficult to read. I recognized this only after seeing various fonts in the large block of text and not initially in the one line option. As with the Bridge debacle, all was not lost. I utilized quite a few of those other fonts as chapter headings or as titles.

Finally I selected Baskerville Old Face as the font for *Haints*. It worked beautifully within the whole. I loved it. It gave a solid representation of the text without overdoing it. There comes a point when design features will no longer enhance a text, but detract from it. I thought I had found a nice equilibrium with the font. However, Baskerville Old Face did not have an italics case in our program. Roadblock number one: This was problematic because the Prologue and Epilogue utilized italics, as well as smaller sections within the text. At this point, I felt a bit foolish for selecting a font without italics. How could I have not noticed that? However, there was a font within that font family that did have the italics case: Baskerville. It changed the length, look, and feel of the novel but not to the point where I felt a need to redesign the chapter headings and the southern gothic motif.

The font not having italics was just one issue working with *Haints*, as it was my first interior. We wanted to make sure we employed the Optical Margin Alignment option. If a sentence begins with a quotation mark, the quotation mark should not be aligned where the first character normally would be on the indent. Rather, with Optical Margin Alignment on, the quotation mark at the beginning of the sentence or at the end of a line is pushed slightly into the margin. Here is an example from *Haints*:

Optical Margin Alignment Off:
"I guess he didn't know many farmers. Too much rain at the wrong time can wash out a whole season of work."
Mary Jean ignored him.

Optical Margin Alignment On:

"I guess he didn't know many farmers. Too much rain at the wrong time can wash out a whole season of work."
Mary Jean ignored him.

Although a small aesthetic feature, the Optical Margin Alignment feature produces a much neater and more precise design over pages of text. That being said, I originally forgot to employ Optical Margin Alignment after placing all the chapters and fixing the widows and orphans. In reviewing the *Haints* third draft, I realized I did not do this. When I turned on the Optical Margin Alignment, this changed the paragraph and sentence lengths, recreating the widows and orphans. This meant going through all the chapters once again, and fixing the issue (like my original debacle with place and autoflow, much of my first experience required extensive revision and waste of time.)

Now, if you are asking what are widows and orphans, that is not entirely a bad thing. In regards to interior design, if I never see a widow or orphan again, I'll be a happy designer. A widow is a paragraph in which the last line runs onto another page, leaving one line at the top of a page before a new paragraph. For example:

You do not want a paragraph to go on and on until the very last line ends
[page break]
on the other page.

In order to remove a widow I would either decrease or increase the kerning of the paragraph. Kerning is the space between letters. By decreasing the space between letters, the paragraph shrinks in size and will pull up onto the same page. Increasing the space between letters will increase the length of the paragraph and may push that widow into a second line, eliminating the widow.

Orphans are handled similarly and are what you call the last word of a paragraph hanging on its own line. For example:

You do not want your sentence to have one word on the last line of paragraph.

Sometimes kerning does not fix the issue, or else it creates text that is too cramped or extended.

Cramped:
In order to remove this problem I would either decrease or increase the kerning of the paragraph. Kerning is the space between letters. By decreasing the space between letters, the paragraph shrinks in size and will pull up onto the same page. Increasing the space between letters will increase the length of the paragraph.

Extended:
In order to remove this problem I would either decrease or increase the kerning of the paragraph. Kerning is the space between letters. By decreasing the space between letters, the paragraph shrinks in size and will pull up onto the same page. Increasing the space between letters will increase the length of the paragraph.

When kerning by itself does not work, I changed the size of the font on a percentage level. This increases or decreases the size of the letters. The process can be risky, for a small variation becomes noticeable juxtaposed with the rest of the text. Often a combination of kerning and font size manipulation is used to remove tricky orphans and widows. Rarely is any difference from non-manipulated text noticeable; however, texts with a lot of dialogue that run about the length of one line, or really short paragraphs provide special difficulties. Another thing to keep in mind when fixing widows and orphans is the rest of the text and where you want your chapter to end, recto or verso (right or left side). You may want to increase/ decrease multiple paragraphs to keep a cohesive transition between the end of one chapter or section and the beginning of another— the chapter starting on the recto and ending on the verso. I did not succeed at this in the six books, but this is a newer revelation and is something to look for in the upcoming manuscripts.

Another issue I had with *Haints* was not labeling and keeping track of my paragraph styles. Within the major block of text, the narrative, I incorporated four different paragraph styles: first paragraph of chapter, main text paragraph, section break, and section break paragraph. The followiong examples are from *Haints*.

First Paragraph of Chapter

D eep in the hole of his own digging, Herb Gatlin mopped the sweat from his leathered neck with a frayed blue handkerchief and offered up a prayer of thanksgiving: another day half done, and he still hadn't taken a drink, cursed God for the pain in the stump of his leg, or killed Doc McKinney.

Main Text Paragraph

The strength to resist the latter was his greatest blessing, and he knew not to take it for granted. He'd fought the murderous urge for twenty years, and so far he'd held his ground, but that didn't mean he could relax his vigilance. The Devil was a relentless foe . . .

Section Break Paragraph

He felt better once they were out in the open air. The day was springlike, breezy and cool, with a blue sky and the first buds bursting on the trees. He was amazed at how much storm debris still cluttered the streets.

Section Break

After *Haints,* once I picked the font size, indentation, drop caps, and character style I wanted, I labeled each paragraph style. Not doing so in *Haints* led to great confusion. I had more than twenty different paragraph styles, labeled only as "paragraph style 1" through "paragraph style 20-something." When I stepped away from the project for a week, I could not remember what paragraph style was for what section. Throwing in acknowledgments and front matter, the styles became a chore to run through and made it difficult to keep the text cohesive. Good housekeeping is a major issue.

What I have found fascinating with designing an interior is the exactness that is necessary within the creative development. Although there is the contemplation of what font would work best with the mood, tone, spectacle, and time period of a text, the most important part is the detailed application of the ideas. I enjoyed measuring out the text boxes, creating a cohesive design that can be replicated chapter after chapter. That being said, the first thing I noticed with *Haints* is that the three tornadoes I designed and inserted into the text to signify the end of a chapter and specific point of view, are off center to the right, albeit minimally. This occurred when I duplicated my main text paragraph styling with a 1p6 indent (the amount of space at the beginning of the text paragraph on the first page) on the first line and then centered it. Although it appears to be centered, it is not. What I should have done was duplicate the section break paragraph for the section break, because the section break paragraph does not have an indent on the first line and thus would have the precise center alignment.

🌪 🌪 🌪

versus

🌪 🌪 🌪

Again, good housekeeping fixes this.

One thing that did work well with *Haints,* however, was the Master Pages function. Once I created a decent page design—what I wanted on the recto and verso running heads (the title of the chapter, author name, book title that appears at the top of the page) and where I wanted it, as well as page numbers—I created a Master Page. I used the initial master as the first chapter (or short story). From there I duplicated that Master Page and changed the recto to show the new chapter or story title. I then applied that Master Page to the second chapter. I did this for each chapter. This method of organization made the running heads easy to keep track of, in my mind anyway. It also kept each page cohesive from one section to another. There may be a better way to do it, but this way worked well for me.

***

Precision within prose is important, but even more so with poetry. I was familiar with prose; I have read many books, had many books to look over and critique, analyze, and emulate. However, designing poetry might as well have been trying to design a likeness to Rembrandt. For this I visited Tammaro. I told him that I was beginning work with *And Then*, a collection of poems by Tim Nolan. I had a few questions with the manuscript that I wanted cleared up with Nolan, so I had sent him an e-mail before my meeting with Tammaro. Nolan confirmed that the poems in the manuscript were correct, that the space between lines should be there.

When I sat down with Tammaro, he mentioned a similar thing, but went into detail about why it should be that way: The open space is part of a poem. This arrangement is both similar and unlike prose. While in prose you look for a font and paragraph style that allows for an easy reading experience—one that allows the subconscious to move seamlessly from word to word, line to line, page to page with a sense of progress at the same time—while a poetry collection needs more attention to the specific poem. All poems within a collection should not be read similarly, by intent of the author. Design should reflect the individual poem's as best as possible, while still holding to a cohesive element within the collection. So, taking each poem as its own entity is one important feature we discussed. The open space allows for a moment of reflection of the line, within the immediacy of the poem as it's being read, and not just at the end. So while one poem may have short lines, another may run more like a prose form. Line breaks matter greatly.

The first aspect of designing a collection of poetry is the margin width within the document set-up page. To increase white space of the collection, I increased the margin width for the collection of poems. From here I created, like prose, differing Master Pages for the varying styles of poems; this can be done only after reading the manuscript and looking at the different styles and types of poems the author has produced. I may not have given the poems the appropriate individual thought by allotting them into Master types, yet doing so allowed for cohesiveness. Specific widths and variations remained within the text as a whole, although they did vary a bit from one poem to the next. The variations were still reflected similarly within the different Master Pages: The longer-lined poems were formatted a certain way, while I gave greater white space to the left margin of the shorter poems.

Another thing Tammaro and I discussed was bringing an element of design from the cover and carrying it through the interior. For *And Then*, Nolan took a beautiful picture that he wanted on the cover. After the cover designer formatted the photo, I took the image, inverted it, and placed it as part of the collection. In looking at *And Then* now, the idea was a good one. My main struggle with placing the picture was determining how I wanted the picture to be seen: how dark, how light. I spent a good amount of time changing the color density of the cover photo before selecting and implementing what is now seen in *And Then*. The photo allows for a common thread to be woven throughout the collection, like the font from the cover; however, the photo on the interior, if I were able to do it again, would be a few shades lighter or become lighter as the collection progressed.

Tammaro also mentioned something that I have taken along with me in the process: simplicity. The design should be simple and allow the reader to experience the text on the page to the highest degree. He also pointed me in the direction of a few publishers that do this well: Graywolf Press, Copper Canyon, and previous collections done by New Rivers Press. I looked through various collections produced by the two other presses and really analyzed the three books that he gave me along with those I found in the New Rivers archive. I found something simple within the texts that I embedded into my designing mind: two varying fonts for the title and the poems, which my mom noticed and appreciated immediately. Some collections used underlines or other little embellishments within the design. I did not think the poems needed something like that, so I chose to stick with a two-font design and a large space between the title and the first line of each poem:

At the River

In my city I walk through the woods

There needs to be a distinction between thoughtful simplicity and simplicity for simpleness's sake. This comes to mind for two different books. Although these books are nice and there are no great design flaws, I still feel a sense of wanting with these books. For *The Way of*

All Flux, I imitated the cover font for the poem titles, as I did with *Good Things*. For these I did not struggle as much for the right font, the right design for each piece. I say this hearing that the books look good, yet something isn't there for me. And this is one of the greatest things I have learned in designing the interior: Do not sell yourself short in what you do. The truth is that the books may be exactly as they should be, yet I did not give them the specific attention to the process that I gave the others, and for that I am lacking. I had a pre-designed template for which I inserted the text, rather than crafting and designing the interior for each title. A sense of diligence and contemplation is missing. They are, for me, books that are half complete, and that eats at me.

So you have considered the manuscripts, selected the right design, font, and removed orphans and widows. Now what? You're done? No. Paper color matters. In looking at the design and readability, you must understand the contrast of the specific font you choose and its appearance on the particular page. Some fonts are heavier and more stark than others; these fonts, when put on a white paper, appear enboldened and stand out too much in contrast with their background. For *It Takes You Over*, we used beige-colored paper, or, to be exact, Natural paper. The combination of the paper color and the font looks exquisite and calm next to the similar font and the white page of *Good Things*. It is my opinion that *Good Things*, as well as *American Fiction Volume 12*, should have been made in that off-white color. This is troublesome from a designer's eyes, but won't affect the reader to a huge degree; however, it is room for improvement. *Haints* works well with the white pages of the interior as the white is reflective of a coloring within the title as well as being a backdrop to a lighter and more subdued font type. Like being aware of the ending and starting of chapters, paper color is something I've only just begun to take into account.

***

There you go, a beginner's guide to designing an interior, by a beginner. As I sit and relay what it's like designing an interior, I feel like I have barely scratched the surface of what I have learned and contemplated. I cannot emphasize enough the support and help with the process I received from the different faculty members and those associated with New Rivers Press. After a year and one set of books, I learned that mistakes happen along the way and that what seemed insurmountable at one time is just a step of the process. Once you complete a project, there is a new one waiting for your attention. At one time in the spring I thought, it is like rolling a rock up a hill, only to have it come back down. In the grind, you can feel like Sisyphus rolling his rock. But take pride when you reach the top of the mountain and in the steps that you took to get there. In speaking of what it's like designing the interior of a book, trying to get the perfect blend of style and precision, I like to use a quote by Albert Camus from his *Myth of Sisyphus*: "The struggle itself towards the heights is enough to fill a man's heart." Although the end results are nice, the discussion and the act of doing was what I remember most fondly and look forward to again.

Besides, when you get the finished copy of a book in your hands, on the first page you turn to, you will likely see that you misspelled the title of a chapter in the running head. Take solace that it wasn't just you that missed the mistake in reviewing, and that others will, hopefully, glance past it. But beware: The error will stand as a reminder of our fallibility every other page of the chapter, which will seem to stretch on and on and never end.

Students from the spring 2013 Introduction to Publishing course take a tour of the warehouse at Itasca, a distribution company located at the BookMobile site. Photo by Suzzanne Kelley.

HALEY FROST

Haley Frost is a photographer and designer and a recent BFA graduate from Minnesota State University Moorhead. While a student, she designed the cover for Rare Earth. *Her design received the American Inhouse Design Award Certificate of Excellence.*

Designing a Book Cover

*D*esigning a book cover isn't as easy as it sounds. There is a lot of preparation and planning that has to happen before the pencil even touches paper, so what you may have thought to be a no-brainer project, actually has a lot of complexity. I spent a semester working with the New Rivers Press creatives on *Rare Earth,* by Bradford Tice, and from that experience I've picked up a few lessons I can now apply to my life after college. A few of those lessons being how print works, how to collaborate with people who aren't familiar with your trade, how to creatively brainstorm utilizing all of the group's brain power, and how to turn that brainstorming power into an effective design. I highly recommend a project like this to those who are aspiring designers because it's not often you get a chance to design for a book that gets published and, hey, that's pretty darn cool. Plus you get to learn something about the printing process and that's unbelievably important to your success as a designer.

There are a lot of things about the publishing and printing processes that I wish I would have understood before taking on this project, but I'm grateful for the experience that I had. I've always struggled to understand poetry, and so you might think that would have had a vastly negative impact on the cover, but a large part of the success of my design came out of the group sessions I participated in. Sure, I could have made a cool looking cover that may or may not have been relatable, but if there's no meaning or reference to the story, is there really a point? Thankfully, the meetings helped keep me on the right track.

We would congregate in different creative groups a few times throughout the semester to discuss our progress, dissect our designs, and more importantly, to go over underlying meanings within the manuscript. As a team, we made discoveries about the writing and about what direction the cover should go. We each had our own strengths and weaknesses, which, in my opinion, makes for the best critiques. My exposure to this method had a large part in molding and shaping my habits as a designer as well as challenging me to think more critically about my work when I meet with clients.

What made this project so interesting was that I had very little interaction with the actual author of the book. He and the staff of New Rivers Press would correspond via e-mail when his opinion was needed but other than that I flew blindly. It was as terrifying as it was liberating and as odd as that sounds, I think what drove me to do this project was the chance to show my author a visual representation of the hard work he had done. I had an opportunity to give his book a voice through the use of visual stimulation. I used interesting typography, bold colors, a lot of texture and mixed them all together to make a cover that would speak to people immediately. I didn't want them to be able to put the book down.

Going back to what I said earlier, I wish I had had more printing experience before participating in this project. I know there would have been many opportunities to make quick improvements in my design and also to understand how to create a file that was 100 percent print ready. Now that I work in an industry specifically driven by printing, I've come to appreciate all of the hard work Al (Professor Allen Sheets) put into making sure my cover would print without error. It's important to understand your craft, and know it well, and I'm glad I know that now. Familiarizing yourself with how to properly prepare files will save both time and money, because once a student has left the cozy, warm blanket of college, people are less likely to lend a helping hand for free.

A few helpful tips I can give to the designers who are reading this is to research print, understand the fundamentals, and talk to a printer. Find out whatever you can about the process and go visit a printing plant; there's no reason not to. There is an unbelievable amount of knowledge there that you can soak up and sponge into your own design that will put you ahead, and if knowledge is wealth, you've just hit the mother-lode. What you learn from those experiences might also play a huge role in what separates you from the next designer when you're fighting to land a job. Establishing a good working relationship with a trustworthy printer will also make projects much easier. Print is almost limitless, especially with today's technology, so why let your growth as a designer be stunted by over-looking it?

You shouldn't. Print is essential, there's no denying that, but what's equally important is how to brainstorm creatively. It's one thing to conceptualize individually, but conceiving a plan in a group of people with different strengths and weaknesses can be a challenge. My experience with New Rivers Press helped me to identify my role in a creative team quickly so I can spend more time listening and evaluating. For designers listening is crucial, and to be frankly honest, I had to learn that lesson the hard way. While working on my project, I didn't spend enough time hearing what the other creatives had to say and it cost me precious design time later. I had to go back and read through notes I took to try to piece together concepts that had already been brought up that I had heard, but truly had not *listened to*.

Once I realized how closely correlated listening and success were, I knew that I had to make adjustments to my routine if I wanted to create good, effective design. I would define effective design as something that encapsulates a little bit of each person's ideas. That way, everyone feels some kind of ownership towards the design and they will take more responsibility in engaging in its development. After this experience, it's been my theory that a group will be more willing to pour their heart into a project if they feel they are accountable for its success. It's a theory that seems ridiculously obvious but it's so easy to get lost in the excitement of designing. It has become common practice for me to insert breakpoints in my design process to make sure that I keep the interest of the group at the heart of every project. If the project doesn't seem to fit those interests, it needs to be redirected back on the right track or thrown out and replaced with something new.

It's been more than a year since I completed my design for *Rare Earth*. A lot of the details have left my mind now, but what I remember are the aspects from the project that I've built upon and incorporated into my career as a graphic designer. The experience of working with the creative minds at New Rivers Press is one that I won't forget because it forced me to take the crucial steps toward becoming a better artist.

JOYCE SUTPHEN

The Bright Obvious

As predicted, it stood there in the morning
bright and clear, although the question we asked

was gone now, and it was much colder—rain
turned to ice. I made a list . . . and coffee too.

I thought about the birds at the feeder last week:
pairs of cardinals, blue jays, woodpeckers,

dozens of chickadees, and sparrows. Where do
the birds go when the wind shakes the branches

like a housemaid with a rug? Perhaps
I should say the obvious thing now,

something like it seems we've lost our way,
and now, I notice the first new snow flakes

and how bright they are as they fill the air,
how soon they will cover everything.

Katie Baker fulfilled all requirements to earn the Certificate in Publishing while working on her English Education degree at MSUM. As an intern, she accessioned a box full of documents from New Rivers Press's past life.

Mystery History Box

On the 27th of August, I took my first professional step into the office of New Rivers Press. Dr. Suzzanne Kelley provided a five-minute general tour of the workplace and listed her expectations and hopes for me as a fall intern. She then told me, in that excited voice that she gets, that the press received a donation. She stepped aside and gestured to a medium-sized, worn box in the corner that seemed to be waiting patiently, slightly slouched to the left.

"This is your first project," she said with a large, happy smile. On the top of the box, thick black marker spelled out the name Robert Alexander.

I had not a simple clue of what to expect from the Robert Alexander Mystery Box. The paper pile of contents seemed endless, like the rope of colorful scarves that the magician pulls out of his sleeve that keeps on coming and coming. Four weeks later, through trials and triumphs (yes, I am slightly exaggerating), I was not only satisfied with my organization of the donation, but I was also honored to have had the privilege. I now have in my brain a plethora of tidbits and tassels of New Rivers Press from the years 1990 to 1999.

I found inside the Alexander Box one decade's worth of fiascos and finances contrasted with excitements and accomplishments. The findings from the contribution range further than that, though. Many of the lessons learned are lessons that still are applicable today. Although the channels of communication have changed a bit, the actual attitudes and rules of communication are still crucial in today's press.

For instance, my first day at New Rivers, I stepped into the office as a rookie and it scared the pants off me. I figured that I would be one of those annoying and ignorant young'ens that is more of an obligation than a use. Rifling through the Alexander Box revealed to me a special thing: I should not be afraid, unless I get a little bit too involved. Interns are helpers, not annoyers. I found this out as I read multiple minutes of meetings. People wanted to perhaps expand the staff and hire a product coordinator or an administrative assistant or editorial assistant because demands for each job were growing heavy. Toward the end of the decade, the press found that interns are efficient, cheap, and save some hassle. There was no need to hire another staff member when interns are willing and able.

Another lesson I can apply to my own life is that it is best to talk about things. In the words of Carol Fisher Saller, author of *The Subversive Copy Editor*, "Keep no secrets." In the Alexander Box, I found that each year, it seemed that the monthly meetings were the glue of the press. Everything was discussed and each person got a chance to voice an opinion. People have to talk, negotiate, and even argue to end either at odds or agreements in order to establish progress in anything. Without the face-to-face communication that the meetings offered, pieces of puzzles would be missed, notions would not be taken as seriously, and some input may not have been heard at all. All sorts of small arguments between staff and affiliates arose because of not taking the time and effort to talk about particulars at hand.

I'm not going to mention names, firstly because the situation is relevant with or without names, and secondly because I do not have permission and I am not going to ask permission because the example is well enough without. There was an e-mail conversation that occurred that had negative tones splattered all over. The issue at hand was whether or not to hire actors to read the works of authors. An e-mail was sent, asking for input. No responses were heard, and if they were, they weren't exactly included in the decision to allow authors' works to be read aloud by actors. Two individuals e-mailed back after the readings, outraged. One who opposed the reading was an author; the other was a very interactive affiliate. Accusations were made, apologies were offered (and not exactly accepted), and the whole staff heard about it. Unfortunate feelings whirled about and it all could have been avoided.

Which brings me to another pattern I realized as I tackled the Alexander Box: Time is of utmost importance. Every e-mail conversation was conducted in a timely matter; repliers replied within a day, and senders sent e-mails a decent time before the mentioned event or plan or request. If, for some reason or another, the replier was a day past due to reply, the message always began with an "I apologize for not reaching you sooner" or a more familiar note, "Thank you for the prompt message, I wish I could have the work ethic you do!"

When I was younger, I absolutely loathed the subject of history. I would hassle my history teacher, "Why the heck do we have to learn history?" His response was always the same, "We learn from it. And if you ask me that question again you're out of here."

The response truly fits in with New Rivers Press. Just as we learn from our mistakes, we learn from history. Flipping through the papers of history I often found myself laughing out loud and thinking, *Wow, I bet this doesn't happen ever again!*

It would be a dumb shame to repeat some of the accidents that occurred in the '90s. One example that comes to memory is the case of an employee. You folks think New Rivers has it tough nowadays? Try March 1996, a major pothole in New Rivers history.

It came to the attention of the staff that they needed to expand the number of workers. So, we hired a qualified man as Executive Director for the press in 1994. His salary was partially funded by a substantial grant.

When the staff hired a marketing assistant, the ED had to undergo a review of his work proficiency. There was little communication and effort from the ED to raise money to pay for the portion of his salary that wasn't covered by the grant. After his review, the board voted to "reduce the Executive Director's position to half-time based on that evaluation" (Board Meeting July 1995). Cutting the ED's work cut his medical insurance along with his hours. The decision violated the man's rights. He sued and won. Along with the ED's reduction in hours came two resignation letters; one was the president of New Rivers Press, the other from an accountant/law servicer. A little less than a year later, New Rivers was ordered to pay $18,000 to the former ED, which drastically added to the financial ouch the press was in.

To add to the impact of this backset, New Rivers' sales were falling behind in numbers due to their then distributor. Before New Rivers partnered with Consortium (our distributor today), we were partnered with a different distribution company. As always, there was a contract of agreement between the two, yet the distributor was falling behind in payments to New Rivers. At first, New Rivers manager Phyllis Jendro wrote explaining that there was money owed, which at that point was not a ton of money, but still something significant.

It turned out that New Rivers was not the only place upset with said distributor. A different press was already on the way to creating a chain e-mail for people that were owed money and ticked off. The debt owed to New Rivers racked up to $11,333 by 1996. Eventually, as in most of these situations, the money was paid back.

When looking into Consortium, no risks were taken. Staff members went to tour Consortium, referrals were made, and records were reviewed. The press did full research on their new distributor and communicated thoroughly in order to avoid mishaps. I suppose it was kind of like falling in love. New Rivers Press got stung by their previous distributor, so it took some time and patience to partner up and trust again. Consortium has proven to be a loyal and stable distributor for sixteen years.

Now I'll tell you about my favorite fiasco. Finding this little tidbit was like finding a ruby in a heap of scrap metal. I knew right when I uncovered the letter that it was something juicy, because it had more than twenty handwritten signatures on the bottom half of it.

The first sentence in the body read, "The English Department of [herein unnamed] University would like to take this opportunity to condemn the criteria that apparently the New Rivers Press has implemented in the manuscript referee process for the Minnesota Voices Project in 1998." *What an intro!*

What is the reasoning behind such a statement? Well, a staff member from said university had submitted an entry for our Minnesota Voices Project, and was shockingly denied. (Again, I don't think naming names would provide any relevancy. If you really want a name, go to the office and check out the Alexander Box archives.) Earlier, I had mentioned that one shouldn't be scared in this business unless they are too involved. This is what I'm talking about. If you get too involved, everything you say is going to follow up. The individual's work was rejected because the judges believed it "covered so-called Big Subjects, like slavery, the Holocaust, rape, AIDS, etc. and that poetry had best avoid such subjects all together." I'm definitely not a super literature guru, so I've never heard of such a thing, but apparently neither had the said university's English Department.

Apologies and defense letters flew around New Rivers for the next few months. The consensus was that the letters that Truesdale had written to the university were in "tactical error" on so-called Big Subjects. A letter was sent from the entire staff to the university English Department in response to the initial anger-letter. The president of New Rivers, Robert Alexander, wrote as follows:

> We would like to take this opportunity to apologize for any misapprehension that may have arisen as the result of Mr. Truesdale's letter to entrants in the MVP competition. I am afraid that Mr. Truesdale inadvertently oversimplified the position of the MVP panelists. The Board of Directors disagrees vehemently with the apparent implications of Mr. Truesdale's letter, that poetry should avoid topics such as the Holocaust. On the other hand, we stand behind our panelists' judgment.

They selected what they felt was the best poetry this year, a complex decision based upon their view of how well an author succeeded in interweaving form and content.

There was no follow-up letter from the university in the Mystery Box.

Now, I know what you're thinking; it's what I'm thinking. *Jeepers, how ugly!* Yes, it's true that we humans remember negative happenings better and more often than the good ones. Although there was a heaping handful of discrepancy in the Mystery Box, there were just as many positive things stacked in the pile.

One positive thing that I've come to appreciate is the man who started all this business. I probably led some of you astray by establishing him as a mistake-maker a few paragraphs earlier. But we've all found ourselves in those icky situations, and Truesdale corrected and apologized for his accidental oversimplification.

My actual introduction to Bill Truesdale starts here. The guy looks a bit goofy, a long-term Coca-Cola addict would be my guess. Well, that was my first impression when I discovered a 1991 article from the *Minneapolis Star Tribune*, which would have been written when Truesdale was sixty-three. As I looked at the black and white picture of the laughing man with soft but acute eyes, I wondered *how the heck did he survive the moves?* He moved from Nyack, New York, to Manhattan to the Twin Cities in '78. At age sixty-three, Truesdale looked as if he was, well, an average sixty-three old.

His features weren't the only things that gave off a silly tint. I got an understanding that this man was somewhat of a joker as I read the publication. According to this particular article, Truesdale's hobbies included travel, carpentry, and "trying to sell his Ph.D. diploma." It goes on to include his description of Nyack as "a town full of Victorian houses and dead people," which is ironically accurate, if you've been to Nyack.

Also, ironically, due to his age, the author champions Truesdale as the "granddaddy of small press publishing." When we think of a granddaddy, we are inclined to think of a wise, all-knowing geezer. Truesdale suits the stereotype because his work up to that time was thrillingly impressive. Some notable verifications for that opinion include facts that he prompted the publishing of more than two hundred books in his first twenty-four years, he developed the Minnesota Voices Project, was among the first literary book publishers to acquire the 501(c)3 status for a not-for-profit press, and was effective enough to influence New Rivers Press representatives into continuing what he had started in 1968 far after his passing.

What a vision Mr. Truesdale must have had. He started his

ambition with an aged Chandler & Price letterpress from a barn in Massachusetts. As of 1992, he had secured two full time employees: Katharine R. Maehr as managing editor and David Cline as assistant to the editor.

The three employees decided to expand the staff in 1994 (see earlier text) and then Phyllis Jendro was welcomed to join in 1995, an addition that, through my research, had proved to be one of the best decisions the group made.

Looking through the papers, Jendro really must have taken her job seriously and with ambition. As I read through her many e-mails, I noticed that she was thorough and timely, as well as polite and professional. There were at least two topics at hand for each of her inquiries. I tell you, there's not much that proves more annoying than when somebody sends seven different e-mails, each with its important message. I suppose it's even more annoying when the person sending the message has written it in a manner that is undecipherable. Then, you have to use that precious time to e-mail a simple "What do you mean?" while using all self-restriction to not put five exclamation points after it!!!!! No, Jendro handled things well, distributing her ideas and transforming the flow of all communication into a stress-free system. There is no evidence of her ever floundering, while with others that is not the case.

With that in mind, probably the top two most important things I've learned thanks to the Alexander Box were made possible by the examples that made up half of the loose leaves in that cardboard container. I now have an education on how to communicate professionally in a group, from individual to individual, and even from company to company. Being a smaller publishing press with the university to hold hands with, New Rivers Press can be friendly and genuine. I think that notion is something to boast about. OK, so the former unnamed university thinks New Rivers really blows because of the MVP problem, but other than that, the Alexander Box is full of thank-you letters, happy hellos, and even most (not all) of the resignation letters were submitted with gentle feelings. There were a few people who left New Rivers because of things that were said in meetings, but papers from those specific meetings for those conversations are missing from the repertoire. Even when problems did happen, New Rivers Press continued with kindness.

Anyway, I learned how to handle difficult situations in a professional manner. People always say that the best learning is through experience. If I apply that, I suppose that I didn't actually have the experience of communicating but I consumed a ton of it through my eyes.

It's kind of like what I went through at my job over by Dent, Minnesota. I started working in the kitchen of the Galaxy Resort (open for five to six hours at supper time) as a dishwasher and help cooker. For five years I watched the head cook do her thing, and observed other sub-cooks on how they did things, too. Through watching, I understood what to do and what not to do. That's why I'm head cook now. I did not know that experience had multiple layers; experience doesn't need to be hands on—it can be eyes on. So, in the context of working in publishing, I learned how to react and act professionally via letters and e-mails, and how not to as well.

There is one person that I've left out, and now I feel ridiculous about it. The Alexander Box is perhaps the smallest donation that Mr. Robert Alexander gave to New Rivers. I have him to thank not only for allowing me the knowledge I received through his box donation, but also for allowing New Rivers Press's existence. I doubt that any of us would be here if it weren't for this guy's big heart and big interest in the direction of literature.

After finishing my project, I came to recognize something that I hadn't yet understood. The term "small press" in itself is an oxymoron. You come over to the office here at Minnesota State University Moorhead and peek at the findings of the Alexander Box and tell me that it's small. You'd be a liar. The list of accomplishments, the books, when you hold them in your hand, may seem small; it's a rectangle that you can fit in your backpack. But each and every day for each person at New Rivers Press consists of little nuts and bolts that are going into this humongous tractor that's going to till and harvest crops within the literary universe year 'round.

Honestly, I hated books when I came into New Rivers this past August. Now, I will never hate a book again. Even if the book is absolutely horrid inside and out, I know that a large number of people spent at least six months of their brain matter fighting with decisions on why to do it that way.

Another oxymoron is the "not-for-profit" notion. Bologna. It would be much more accurate to say that New Rivers is a "not-for-money" business. Yes, that's much, much more accurate. The profits are huge and are visible in the spirit of New Rivers; the smiles that reappear almost every day (probably not every day because everybody has bad days), the idea that what Truesdale established is not sinking, the news articles that feature the wonders of New Rivers Press, and the students absorbing the details they will pull out later in their careers are a few profits that the press rakes in. The best part is that New Rivers isn't selfish; it shares its profits with the world.

This internship was all just to get a Certificate in Publishing, something that I really didn't need; it was a fancy addition to my major. Inspiration, though, has soaked me to the marrow, and I think perhaps that this business is worth pursuing.

Tarver Nova is a workflow coordinator at Integreon. He completed the Certificate in Publishing during his undergraduate studies, and then later, while an MFA student at University of Southern Maine, completed an internship with New Rivers Press.

The Digital World: A Beginner's Guide to the E-Book Industry

Like music and movies before it, the book has entered its digital revolution. Alongside the hardcover and paperback formats, books now exist in the digital format, as e-books. Readers access e-books through a computer, a tablet, or a dedicated reading device called an e-reader. In the past five years, the United States in particular has seen an explosion of sales of both e-books and the devices on which to read them. According to the International Digital Publishing Forum, US sales of e-books in January 2010 were up almost *quadruple* the year previous, for a profit of $31 million.[1] This trend is continuing; the Association of American Publishers revealed that, as of January 2012, they saw an increase in e-book sales of 73 percent, which translates to a 27 percent increase in revenue.[2]

With the e-book popularity comes the proliferation of e-readers, both new and upgraded; Amazon, Barnes and Noble, and Sony have released a new e-reading device—if not multiple devices—every year since 2009. This, along with dozens of other e-reader start-ups, has sent sales of the readers' "electronic paper" displays soaring by more than 400 percent.[3] Tablets are booming as well. Current predictions estimate that tablet sales will reach an estimated 54 percent increase—to more than 100 million tablets sold in 2012 alone.[4] E-readers and tablets are quickly becoming more widely used, understood, and accepted among readers.

It is now more important than ever for all book-lovers—readers, authors, publishers, and librarians—to come to understand this digital age. E-books are entering into all areas of the book business, even overtaking traditional mediums. In 2010, Amazon announced that sales of e-books outnumbered hardcovers.[5] That same year, Barnes and Noble,

a bookseller long entrenched in the world of physical books, predicted that its market share in digital books (approximately 30 percent) is
more than the 17 percent it holds in the physical book market.[6] And
sales continue to grow. As of 2012, most big-name publishers report
that e-book sales are between 15 and 20 percent of their entire book
sales, up significantly from only a year previous. It's clear: e-book
reading is likely here to stay.

The E-Book Advantage

Though physical books aren't yet going the way of the 8-track, e-books
hold advantages for the reader. There are a few particularly salient reasons to read digitally. E-books are convenient, cheap, and adjustable.

The E-Book Convenience

An e-book can be, in many ways, more convenient than a physical
book. For one, e-readers can store thousands of books on devices that
weigh less than a pound. This is especially handy for travelers, or those
simply wanting to save on space. All a reader's books tend to be
stored on the Internet as well, meaning a reader's library is safe from
flood or fire and is accessible anywhere. And although it's the part
physical-book readers most miss, the lack of pages can be a boon for
people who are bedridden or disabled.

The E-Book Price

E-books currently tend to be priced more cheaply than their print
counterparts. Particularly, e-books have a price advantage over hardcovers; newly-released e-books are often $10 to $15, significantly
more affordable than the average $25 to $35 hardcover. Even the
backlist tends to be cheaper, as trade paperback books priced between
$10 and $16 can be found in e-book for $4 to $9. The only print
book form that matches many e-books is the mass market paperback;
these books tend to be priced around $7.99 or $8.99 for both print
and digital.

The E-Book Adaptability

E-readers often allow changing of the text appearance, so that
reading is best suited for the particular reader. Everything from text
size to font and margins to even background color may be changed.

Although this may seem like a gimmick to the average reader, those with reading difficulties greatly benefit from the customizable text of the e-book.

E-Books: A Short History

Though e-reading is something that has exploded only within the past few years, the concept of e-books is nothing new. In fact, the e-book, in some form or another, has been around for nearly forty years. Investigating the history of e-publishing reveals why only now the market has exploded.

The first general e-books came about from the Project Gutenberg in the early 1970s. The project, which is still active today with a content list of more than 33,000, is a volunteer endeavor to convert books and documents into e-books. Although e-books found limited implementation into early computers, it wasn't until the 1990s that the e-book gained market traction. The first e-readers were created in 1998, but it wasn't until nearly ten years later that the market saw E-Ink, a unique type of screen used in nearly all of today's e-readers.

E-Ink is the proprietary name for an electronic paper display. Unlike most computer screens, E-Ink is not backlit; that is, it doesn't produce its own light. This is ideal in most reading conditions, as the screen is more akin to paper. Many readers report less eyestrain due to the non-backlit screen, and unlike LCD screens, E-Ink can be read in direct sunlight. Sony's PRS-500 e-reader, released in 2006, was the first major e-reader in America with an E-Ink screen. Because of the PRS-500's popularity (attributed in large part to the versatility of the E-Ink screen) more e-readers began to appear on the market. In 2007, Amazon produced the Kindle, the first with an e-book store in the device itself. The year 2009 saw the market accelerate, with Amazon introducing the Kindle 2 and larger Kindle DX, and Barnes and Noble introducing the Nook. Only a year later, Amazon released its third generation Kindle, Sony released three new e-readers, and Apple released the iPad, a tablet computer that can be purposed as an e-reader. Continued iterations of all these devices—plus tablet-like devices from Barnes and Noble and Amazon—have further accelerated this field.

Although dozens of e-readers and e-bookstores have recently saturated the market, the four mentioned companies—Amazon, Barnes and Noble, Apple, and Sony—hold a substantial chunk of the e-book market share. Because of this—and because of e-book format issues addressed later—we will focus only on these four for comparison.

E-Reading Devices: An Overview

Dedicated E-Readers. First covered are the dedicated e-readers—those devices that are, traditionally, E-Ink, single-purpose electronics for reading. These devices tend to be compact and focused, often with six-inch screens and weighing around eight ounces.

Amazon Kindle. Though not the first on the market, Amazon's Kindle has quickly claimed e-book dominance. The Kindle is estimated to hold approximately 60 percent of the e-book market. The Kindle has gone through multiple iterations, with the original Kindle released in 2007 and hardware revisions in 2009, 2010, and 2011. The device links to an online account with Amazon.com. The device connects to the Amazon e-bookstore via Wi-Fi or, optionally, 3G cell signals to purchase and download new books, which are then backed up on the user's Amazon.com account. With this same online account, customers can access their library of purchased books on a PC, Apple product, Blackberry, or Droid phone.

Most notable is Kindle's "Read to Me" feature, which can convert e-books into synthesized speech, making this a particularly useful device for the blind or visually impaired. Publishers dictate whether this feature can be implemented; there are business-wide fears that "Read to Me" is an infringement in audiobook rights, meaning that many books bought on the Kindle cannot be converted to synthesized speech.

Barnes and Noble Nook. Seen as Barnes and Noble's answer to the Kindle, the Nook is also a means for the New York-based bookstore to stay viable as books move digital. Nook retains many of the same features as Kindle, including the onboard e-bookstore and the online library backup. Nook owners can also access their library on all the same devices as Kindle owners.

Most notably, Barnes and Noble leverages its brick-and-mortar stores for Nook, providing in-store support for Nook owners. Along this vein is Nook's "Read in Store" feature, which allows many e-books to be opened cover-to-cover an hour every day when Nook owners are in a Barnes and Noble store.

Sony Reader. Sony carries three different sizes of its e-reader brand, each a different size screen ranging from five-inches to seven-inches diagonally. Most notable is that all three models are entirely touch-screen, using touch or a stylus to navigate menus or turn pages. The Sony Readers cater most to those who established a library of e-books before Kindle came out, as the Sony Readers, unlike Kindle, accept the standard EPUB format as well as the now-outdated LIT format of the early 2000s. As EPUB becomes more ubiquitous, Sony Readers are for those who wish to have an "open-source" library of e-books—that is, a collection of titles bought from many places. With the rise of many e-bookstores such as BooksOnBoard.com or the Google Bookstore, the Sony Readers are gaining an ever-widening selection of titles from companies not trying to support their own e-readers.

Tablets. As of only 2011—mainly driven by the success of the Apple iPad—a large influx of readers are now using tablet computers for their reading needs. This is made easy because Amazon, Barnes and Noble, and Sony—as well as a few others—have all made apps for tablets that allow tablet users to read the respective companies' books. A more diverse reading environment may appeal to readers, though likely the larger draw to tablets is their increasingly multifunctional ecosystems. While this can serve as a distraction to reading, Forrester Research has found at least 31 percent of publishers believe tablets are ideal for reading.[7] As such, the tablets—especially the reading tablets produced by Barnes and Noble and Amazon—are worth investigating.

Apple iPad. Though not a dedicated e-reader in its own right, the Apple iPad has definitely put pressure on dedicated e-readers. Instead of relying on E-Ink, the iPad is a full-color, backlit touch-screen. Both benefits and limitations abound for this screen. The iPad provides a more vivid reading experience with color and the ability to read in the dark, but reading on a backlit screen for extended periods of time bring concerns of eyestrain and battery life. Also, the backlit screen will easily wash out in direct sunlight, while E-Ink stays clear.

For those that need the extra functionality, however, the dedicated e-readers (and their slower E-Ink technologies) tend to be no match. One major appeal of the iPad is its multipurpose use. It serves not only as an e-reader, but as a competent web browser, word processor, and nearly anything a media consumer may need. Here it's focus versus functionality; most e-readers are best for reading, but the iPad is good at nearly everything else.

While the iPad has its own application for e-books, "iBooks," Amazon and Barnes and Noble's apps bring Kindle or Nook e-books on the iPad. In this regard, the iPad may be seen not as direct competition, but as an alternative in the e-reader market. Analysts and journalists alike wonder if the tablet computers like the iPad will kill dedicated e-readers, but a more practical concern for publishers and authors is how iPad's "apps" environment—small, downloadable programs that can add new functionality to the device—will influence the sales of dedicated e-readers and the e-books themselves.

Barnes and Noble Nook Tablet. Perhaps considered a merger of an e-reader and a tablet, Barnes and Noble's Nook Tablet is one of the newest kinds of devices for reading. Form-wise, it's closer to an e-reader; it has a smaller screen than an iPad or most full-fledged tablets, and it's more focused on books. However, it has many of the same features as a tablet; it can browse the Internet, and it has access to apps and games (though not nearly as many as the high-end tablets). All this—plus a much cheaper price tag—makes products like this ideal for readers who need Internet access as well.

Although this tablet-like format brings with it added functionality, the Nook Tablet still centers around reading. The home screen, for example, consists of books, not apps, and the type of LCD used is easier to read than an iPad's. The Nook Tablet's proprietary screen even reads decently in sunlight. Yet it brings with it the same troubles of the iPad—relatively short battery life and possible eyestrain.

Amazon Kindle Fire. Amazon's answer to Barnes and Noble's earlier iteration of the Nook Tablet, the Kindle Fire is another "reading tablet." Like Barnes and Noble, Amazon provides a device that's a middle ground between an e-reader and a tablet. Hardware-wise, the Kindle Fire and the Nook Tablet are nearly identical; the differences are nearly all in the ecosystems. Amazon has a more dedicated focus to non-reading functions like apps and movies, and as such will see more access to that content. However, Amazon's purely online presence again is less appealing for those who want in-store support.

E-Readers Versus Tablets. Although e-reader sales of the past five years have been booming, the proliferation of tablets and smartphones appears to be disrupting the sales of dedicated e-readers. After Christmas 2011, Barnes and Noble reported that demand for the Nook Tablet was greater than expected, but that demand for their dedicated e-reader, the Nook Simple Touch, was significantly less.[8] Likewise, Amazon has evidence that its e-reader sales have also slowed.[9] As Amazon and Barnes and Noble together may hold up to 90 percent of the e-book market—and especially considering each company has not seen decreased sales of their reading tablets—this suggests that readers are beginning to prefer tablet devices.

While there are many other devices on the market, it is only prudent for the publisher or author to watch the four companies mentioned: Amazon, Barnes and Noble, Sony, and Apple. This is not simply because many of these lesser-known devices may die away; on the contrary, there is still potential for new devices to influence the e-reader market. However, nearly all lesser e-readers function in the same file format. For a publisher or author, then, an e-book need only be provided in EPUB format to cover the great majority of the e-reader market. Yet one format alone won't be enough for a small press publisher to thrive: file format for e-books is quickly evolving into a competition in its own right.

E-Book Formats. Like any digital media, e-books are produced in multiple file formats. Different e-readers and computers are capable of reading different formats, and as of yet no one device can natively read all formats. For larger publishers, this variability is of no issue as they have the resources to convert the files into the proper formats for each device. For the small press or independent author, however, converting e-books into correct file formats is critical to getting the book intact in the reader's hands. Incorrect formats may make the device display text incorrectly, or worse, not at all.

An Overview of Frequently Used e-Book Formats

EPUB. EPUB, short for "e-publication," is the de facto standard format of e-books. It was developed by the International Digital Publishing Forum (IDPF), an association created to standardize the digital publishing industry. Most publishers and e-bookstores, including Barnes and Noble and Sony, provide their books in this format. This file format is preferred in publishing to PDF or .doc formats for two main reasons: its adaptability and its metadata capabilities.

EPUB is adaptable in multiple ways. In line with the IDPF's goals, EPUB is a reflowable format. This means the text of an EPUB book can easily be reformatted for the reading device. Margins, page breaks, and even font size and type adjust based on the needs of the reader. An EPUB book is so adjustable, in fact, that publishers have control over which aspects of the book will change across devices. This leaves them with some influence over the book's appearance.

EPUB's adaptability extends beyond simple text formatting, as the file itself can be manipulated based on the needs of the distributor. For example, companies like Barnes and Noble who wish to place copy protection (Digital Rights Management, explained later in this essay) on their titles have programmed their own versions of EPUB, which require proof of purchase if a title is opened on unrecognized devices. Libraries can also leverage the format's adaptability by programming "rentable" e-books, titles that stay on a device for a limited length of time before expiring. This provides libraries with a means to lend out e-books very much like their physical copies.

Another major advantage of EPUB is the existence of metadata. Metadata is a broad term for any information associated with a book that is utilized by the device, rather than displayed in-text. For example, many EPUB books include metadata on the beginning of chapters. This way, the e-reader can display a list of chapter headings so that the user can easily navigate throughout the book.

AZW. While EPUB is meant to be a set standard for e-books, many e-books today are sold in AZW format. AZW is the proprietary format of Amazon's Kindle e-reader. Adapted from another e-book format, MOBI, it has many of the same features as EPUB, including adaptability and metadata. Though functionally there's little difference between EPUB and AZW, small presses and independent authors need to be aware of this separate format. The Kindle, which is currently the most prominent e-reader on the market, uses only AZW, a format that no other device can natively support. Amazon has also chosen not to support EPUB on Kindle. Effectively, this means that e-books bought from other sources cannot be used on Kindle, and vice versa. Thus, a small press must have a means to create both an EPUB and an AZW format of their titles if they expect to distribute through both Kindle and other devices.

PDF. Some publishers, especially those working with works that require complex formatting or many images, will at times opt to publish in PDF (Portable Document Format). However, this format is usually only used for textbooks or a business's internal documents. Although there are more resources to create complex texts with PDF than other e-book formats, PDF is limited in that it does not display as well on e-readers. This is because PDFs tend to be less flexible with reflowing, or adjusting margins, font sizes, or image size. Over time, e-readers will become better suited to read PDF as companies release software and hardware upgrades to their devices, but it's unlikely the publishing industry will adopt PDF as a standard. The format in its current state simply doesn't provide the same capabilities as the afore-mentioned formats, in large part because it is considered a format for *documents*, not books.

It's important to note that most e-reading devices are capable of displaying .doc, .html, or any number of lesser-used e-book files. However, these formats aren't ideal for e-publication. Word document and .html are too loose, allowing the reader to manipulate the text itself. The existence of other e-book formats is essentially a non-issue, at least in the perspective of the publisher, as the major e-readers are capable of either EPUB or AZW.

DRM and Ownership. One hotly contested issue in the e-publishing world is that of Digital Rights Management (DRM). Like many music or video game companies, the largest e-bookstores sell their content with DRM attached. This means that a purchased title can be opened on a limited number of devices, and that the purchaser cannot simply give copies of their e-books to someone else. DRM is found most notably on any books purchased from the Amazon, Apple, and Barnes and Noble e-bookstores.

From the company's perspective, DRM is a defense against piracy and over-sharing. This is especially relevant because of the way e-books are so easily replicated. Unlike a physical book, an owner can give a copy of an e-book to a friend and still own a copy themselves. Digital Rights Management cracks down on this, making it nearly impossible for an individual to open a traded copy of an e-book. Amazon and Barnes and Noble have taken strides to alleviate this; both companies allow a person to link their e-book account to multiple devices. For example, an individual may use a central Amazon or Barnes and Noble account to access the same library of books on the company's e-reader, a PC or Apple product, or a smart phone such as a Blackberry or Android. This is especially useful as it provides the entire personal library to each device simultaneously.

From the consumer's perspective, however, even unlimited personal access can be too limiting. Most noteworthy is that any books bought from Amazon or Barnes and Noble cannot be read on a competitor's e-readers. A Barnes and Noble customer who buys a Kindle, then, cannot easily transfer their titles, nor can they be read on a Sony e-reader.

It is possible, through software, to forcibly remove DRM from e-books bought from Amazon or Barnes and Noble. However, this is considered voiding the terms of use set forth by the companies, and may be considered illegal (though no one has yet been charged in court for DRM removal). Further limiting is the formatting issue, especially for Kindle users. Individuals who convert their library from, say, AZW to EPUB, may find formatting (especially metadata) to be lost in the process, thus hindering the reading process.

Another contentious issue in the e-publishing world is that of ownership. Currently, companies such as Amazon and Barnes and Noble provide their titles under *license*, not ownership. If someone buys an e-book, they often then own the license to read the title. While legally the buyer retains the right to download a local copy of the e-book for his personal use, he does not have the right to give the title to someone else.

In the end, DRM is an imperfect means to address a more fundamental problem: The recent revolutions in digital media have outgrown traditional copyright doctrines. Never before has someone been able to give away music, photos, or books—while *still owning the original copy*. This fundamental difference is a heated issue that legal scholars and the publishing industry are investigating, but for now there is no cut-and-dried answer to the use of DRM.

The Future of the E-Book

Although the world of digital publishing can yet be contentious, there are a number of reasons the e-book has gained market traction. Perhaps the most salient benefit is the portability and storage. Most anyone can see the benefit of carrying around their entire bookshelf with them—and not on rows of heavy *actual* bookshelves. But even those who don't travel find reason to build a digital library. Certainly, there's truth to the print loyalist's claim that a regular book doesn't run out of batteries; however, an e-book doesn't mold, damage, or deteriorate. A reader who returns to an e-book two years after they first read it will find it in the same condition as it began (perhaps in even better condition, as screen technologies continue to improve). And, in the worst of catastrophes, the digital reader's home destroyed by fire means only that the reader has to re-download their titles for free.

And what is the future of the e-publishing world? It's hard to know for sure, but there are speculations. E-readers are expected to continue their rise in popularity, potentially hitting their peak in 2013.[10] Assumedly, after this e-readers will have become so ubiquitous that the market will have no more room for great explosions of growth. Each year, e-reader technology will continue to advance, with leaps in technology occurring practically every six months. The next big innovation will be a new kind of screen—one that has the non-backlit, paper-like qualities of E-Ink, but with the responsiveness (and color) of LCDs.[11] Where the technology goes after that is anyone's guess, considering each technological bound uses the tech before it as a jumping-point.

The digital revolution will continue to influence not only e-readers but also the reading world at large. Advancing technology will open the door for new content—picture books, graphic novels, textbooks, and even multimedia mutations like movie-books have begun to arrive. Independent authors and small presses can now claim a foothold in the leveling force that is the e-market. The book is becoming more interactive. E-readers are becoming common in classrooms, and very likely will supplant laptops and print textbooks in the next few years. Public libraries are lending out e-books alongside their physical copies.

There's no single part of the book world that won't be influenced by digital publishing. Yet perhaps the best news to come out of this development is that reports are suggesting that more people are reading.[12] With nearly all other kinds of media—including movies, music, and video games—moving toward digital distribution, the e-reader serves as a way to bring the modern reader stories in a way most familiar to them. And while we won't likely know for years whether the e-reader will permanently change people's reading habits, at least we can be assured that people still want to curl up to a good (digital) book.

1. Richard Curtis and Jane Friedman, "Open Road Welcomes E-reads Readers and authors," *The Open Road Blog*, 2010. http://ereads.com/2010/03/january-10-e-book-sales-almost.html

2. Aaron Souppouris, "Ebooks, young readers stimulate publishing industry growth, *The Verge*, 2012. http://www.theverge.com/2012/3/30/2913366/ebook-sales-by-demographic-january-2012-aap

3. Display Research, "E-book Popularity Drives Electronic Paper Display (EPD) Shipments to 417% Y/Y Growth." *An NPD Group Company*, 2010. http://www.displaysearch.com/cps/rde/xchg/displaysearch/hs.xsl/100413_e_book_popularity_drives_electronic_paper_display_epd_shipments_to_417_y_y_growth.asp

4. Danielle Kucera, "Tablet Sales Will Soar 54 Percent This Year, IDC Says," *Bloomber News*, 2012. http://www.businessweek.com/news/2012-03-13/tablet-sales-will-soar-54-percent-this-year-idc-says

5. Claire Cain Miller, "E-Books Top Hardcovers at Amazon," *The New York Times Online*, 2010. http://www.nytimes.com/2010/07/20/technology/20kindle.html

6. Larry Dignana, "Barnes & Noble: Nook, e-book sales accelerating," *ZDNet*, 2010. http://www.zdnet.com/blog/btl/barnes-noble-nook-e-book-sales-accelerating/38300

7. Julie Bosman and Matt Richtel, "Finding Your Book Interrupted . . . By the Tablet You Read It On," *The New York Times Online*, 2012. http://www.nytimes.com/2012/03/05/business/media/e-books-on-tablets-fight-digital-distractions.html

8. Dan Mitchell, "Yes B&N, cut the Nook loose," *CNNMoney*, 2012. http://tech.fortune.cnn.com/2012/01/06/bn-cut-the-nook-loose/

9. Eric Savitz, "Amazon: Kindle Demand Weakening? Pac Crest Cuts Views," *Forbes*, 2012. http://www.forbes.com/sites/ericsavitz/2012/03/19/amazon-kindle-demand-weakening-pac-crest-cuts-views/

10. Nick Spence, "E-Reader Sales to Peak by 2013, Report Says," *TechHive*, 2010. http://www.pcworld.com/article/197537/ereader_sales_to_peak_by_2013_report_says.html

11. David Carnoy, "What's next for e-readers: a Mirasol in the making?" *Cnet*, 2010. http://ces.cnet.com/8301-32254_1-20025651-283.html

12. Evann Gastaldo, "E-Readers Read More," *Newser*. 2010. http://www.newser.com/story/98920/e-readers-read-more.html

RYAN CHRISTIANSEN

Ryan Christiansen earned the Certificate in Publishing while completing his MFA in Creative Writing at MSUM. He subsequently founded the e-book-only publishing company, Knuckledown Press. He serves as the associate editor for New Rivers Press's Electronic Book Series.

Crossing the Digital Horizon: The Electronic Book Series

In January 2010, Apple Inc. announced it would produce the first iPad, and as someone who has been following Apple and digital technology trends since the first Macintosh computer emerged onto the scene in 1984, I felt very strongly that this new device would ensure that e-books, as a commodity, would be here to stay, just as the iPod had made digital downloads the preferred format for purchasing music.

I never would have made this same prediction about e-books in 1998, however, when the first wave of e-books and e-readers hit the market, a surge that died quickly and quietly. Most people don't even remember we had e-books before Amazon, and for good reason: The right people weren't involved, namely Amazon's founder and CEO, Jeff Bezos, but also Apple's late founder and CEO, Steve Jobs, who waited to make his move with the iPad until three years after Amazon had first introduced the Kindle. It seems 2010 was the time when consumers were finally ready to get on board with e-books.

Or were they?

In 1998, Jobs told *BusinessWeek* that "a lot of times, people don't know what they want until you show it to them," and so perhaps it takes a showman, or at least someone who knows a good product when he imagines it, to get people on board. You could argue that Jobs was the premier digital showman of his time, masterfully coordinating press conferences to unveil the new products that he intuitively knew people would want (iPhone, anyone?). And so on that cold day in January when Jobs announced the iPad, I suggested, without hesitation, that New Rivers Press should get into e-books, too.

But it hasn't been easy.

When we first started publishing our books as e-books (in addition to print), we learned that producing e-books can be expensive.

We came to understand that because we operate in a print-first publishing environment, we have to pay our printer hundreds of dollars per title to convert our print-ready files to e-book files, a task that requires taking a page layout format in Adobe InDesign and converting it backward to a text-flow format in Microsoft Word. It's a process akin to stitching together individual pages to make a scroll, and it seems counterproductive because, after all, a book typically starts out as a manuscript in Microsoft Word or in another compatible word processor.

I knew there had to be a less expensive and easier way to publish e-books.

To prove my point, I started my own e-book-only literary press, Knuckledown Press, in 2011, and within a year I'd published several books, all by myself. And during the entire editing and publishing process, I never left Microsoft Word. I learned first-hand how quickly and cost-effectively a literary press could publish books in the e-book format, and that's when I suggested New Rivers Press should start an e-book-only series, too, and so we started the New Rivers Press Electronic Book Series—with reservations.

For one, we knew the Electronic Book Series would have to be clearly different from the Many Voices Project, and so instead of soliciting manuscripts with a heavy literary focus, which tend to be genre-neutral, for the Electronic Book Series we sought to publish popular fiction titles with literary value in the genres of Fantasy, Horror, Mystery, Romance, Science Fiction, Thriller/Suspense, Westerns, Young Adult, Inspirational, and all sub-genres.

A second reservation we had was giving books in the e-book-only series the same ethos that our other books carry. Therefore, to set the Electronic Book Series apart, we adopted an older version of the New Rivers Press logo as the basis for a new logo for the series. Each Electronic Book Series e-book now carries that logo in a banner across the cover, along with the author's name.

With these criteria in hand, in the summer of 2012 we solicited manuscripts for the Electronic Book Series, and I spent the next several months reviewing submissions on Submittable.com, the online submissions service we determined would be the sole method for submitting manuscripts to the series. When I'd whittled the number of manuscripts under consideration down to a handful, I forwarded the manuscripts from Submittable to my Amazon Kindle, where I completed my evaluation. In the spring of 2013, after several weeks of editing and preparing promotional material, I published our first title, *Principles of Navigation*, a literary romance by Peter W. Fong.

So, piece of cake. Right?

Well, from a technical standpoint, yes. Publishing an eBook-only series has proven to be easy to manage: Authors submit online, editors review online, editors and authors negotiate contracts by e-mail, editors copyedit the books in Microsoft Word, authors negotiate copyedits in the same environment, and we publish the books using Amazon's web-based Kindle Direct Publishing system. And readers purchase the book online. There is no distributor for the e-books because we deal directly with Amazon. The entire process remains digital, and even though we say that we *published* a new book for the world to enjoy, we never actually *printed* anything, not even the manuscript.

Challenges remain, however. Authors (more than readers, it seems) want something tangible to hold onto when they get published. This is hard for me to understand because I'm an editor who believes that the literary value of a work should supersede any commercial value, and that we shouldn't be so concerned about the physicality of our work, that it's what's inside a book—the words—that really count.

However, authors tend to want both the tangibles and the intangibles that go along with having a *printed* book published: They want an object they can show to other people, much like keeping the head of an animal in a trophy room. And if they work in academia, they want the publishing ethos that historically goes along with having a published, *printed* book. And there is the perceived durability of a printed book, and the fact that printed books facilitate face-to-face interactions between authors and readers. I get it: You can't hold an e-book, and holding an e-reader is like holding a portal to a book, and not the book itself.

The best we can do in terms of tangibility is to provide authors with postcards, perhaps with QR codes so that readers can quickly access and purchase books online. And instead of face-to-face interactions, e-book-only authors must focus on connecting to readers through the virtual world of social networking, e-mail, and blogs. The context is different.

As for credibility, New Rivers Press has an established ethos in the publishing industry, so that authority should transmit automatically to e-books. And as for durability, e-books have a different *kind* of robustness than printed books because you can easily sell e-books all over the world, in an instant.

Printing books in the hopes that you can sell them is a huge investment (some call it speculation), and small literary presses need philanthropic donations to survive. But we want to thrive. The Electronic Book Series allows us to bring more worthy titles to the marketplace, titles we wouldn't be able to publish in print, simply due to cost.

Early on, some of my cohorts paled at the idea we might publish something as ephemeral as the digital book. But that was four years ago now, a lifetime in the digital age, and today, New Rivers Press and our readers have embraced the e-book. It's worth noting that nowadays, authors *expect* their books will be published in the e-book format, and most of all, they want their work to reach an audience. The quickest way to an audience is through the e-book marketplace.

THOM TAMMARO

Thom Tammaro is the author of two poetry collections and co-editor of three award-winning anthologies. Tammaro, along with Joyce Sutphen and Connie Wanek, co-edited To Sing Along the Way. *He serves as New Rivers Press's poetry coordinator, and he is currently working with Debra Marquart on a poetry collection we will publish in 2015.*

For Your Consideration:
Some Thoughts on Small, Independent
Publishing in America

For the past nine years, I have been invited to speak with the students in ENGLISH 402/502 Introduction to Publishing, the gateway course to MSUM's Certificate in Publishing. Original-ly, I was asked to speak about the history of small and independent press publishing in America. Daunted by that charge, I drew upon my self-directed and not-so-methodical research and reading about the topic, but perhaps more so, I drew upon my own experiences as a teacher/writer/editor/publisher involved in the community of small press publishing and publishers and university presses for nearly three decades—as a small press editor and publisher during the mid-1970s and 1980s; as a writer and editor published by small presses and university presses; and again as a small press editor when I served as interim senior editor at New Rivers Press in 2003-2004, when Alan Davis was on sabbatical leave; and my eight years as poetry editor for New Rivers Press. While I understood that my focus might narrow the scope of my presentation, I also believed that I could offer students the perspective of someone "in the trenches," and since I knew many students were about to make that same leap—or were at least contem-plating the idea—I thought this perspective might be helpful to them.

Each time I meet the class I announce that the views expressed are those of the speaker, and that if they are still interested in the topic after my presentation that they should explore it on their own, perhaps beginning with the help of the selected bibliography I provide them. And I also suggest that they, too, should jump into the small press publishing trenches, just as I did back in the mid-1970s, mostly na-ive but with abundant youthful energy. No doubt, many of them have this in mind by the time they complete the certificate, and I know several who have gone on to do just that by starting their own magazines, e-zines, and small presses. For better or worse, I am there to encourage them to do so.

What I offer in this essay, then, is a written version of the presentation I give to the Intro to Publishing class each spring semester. Over the years, I have modified and updated my talk as needed (yes, accompanied with PowerPoint slides since the beginning), to reflect continual changes brought about by the tsunamis of technology and the rise in e-publishing, as well as my own constantly rebalancing notions and ideas about the nature of small, independent publishing. The following five topics—or "considerations" as I label them on my PowerPoint slide—guide my presentations: Technology, Government Funding, The Reagan Era and the Small Business Model, Markets & Distribution, and The Future. In my informal presentation to the class, national and personal history often intersect like that aggregate point in a Venn diagram.

Certainly there are as many approaches to the topic as there are presenters, but the considerations that I have chosen allow me to place information and perspective on the table for the students that, in turn, allows them to enter the conversation and wrestle with some of the issues, dynamics, challenges, and opportunities offered by small, independent publishing.

Before I talk about the five considerations, I spend a little time trying to define small press and independent publishing. If you research these terms, you'll find their definitions somewhat mercurial, depending upon the criteria being used. Using a yearly operating budget as a criteria, for example, I've found sources that define small press as any press with a budget of less than $1 million dollars, and others who say $50,000 or less defines a small press. Another criterion is the number of books published in a fiscal year—again, I've seen figures ranging from forty books published to less than ten per year. Other measures include number of paid staff members and IRS tax status (for profit or not-for-profit 501(c)3 status). I ask students to consider the idea of "small" in relationship to what—large presses? For-profit presses such as HarperCollins? Alfred A. Knopf? Random House? Is a press that is started for the purpose of publishing one's own poetry a "small press" in the same way that New Rivers Press, Coffee House Press, Copper Canyon Press, or Graywolf Press are small presses? As a rule of thumb, I suggest students look at a press's self-description, mission, and especially to look for the words "independent" and "not-for-profit." These parameters more often than not distinguish a press more for its mission and scope, than they do a press's budget, staff size, or titles in print.

I also discuss the many distinctions that exist, for better or for worse, for the kinds of publishing that are available: vanity publishing, self-publishing, cooperative publishing, independent publishing, niche publishing, micro-publishing, etc. A recent trend I've noticed is the use of the word "independent" for "self-publishing." As technology and social media offer new ways to produce and market books, the lines are blurring, since all of the above types of publishing may use the same technology and services such as Print-on-Demand (POD) printing services. One question that gets discussion going is "What is the difference between a printer and a publisher?" And speaking of self-publishing, the stigma previously associated with "self-publishing" (especially in academic circles) seems to be eroding with the Millennial generation, who seems less concerned with how something is published. *Library Journal* explores this phenomenon in detail in a recent article, "What's the Problem with Self-Publishing?" by Josh Hardo (11 April 2013). Written for librarians primarily, the article provides excellent insight into the ever-growing phenomenon of self-publishing.

I could spend a lot of time discussing the variations and nuances of these types of publishing, but I choose not to; however, I do feel obligated to mention them since the students no doubt will encounter the terms and language—or at least experience the phenomena—if and when they decide to enter the worlds of small or commercial publishing.

***

To say that technology has affected and shaped the world of small, independent publishing is to state the obvious. Just as technology has influenced and shaped every other facet in the rise and fall of human civilization, it certainly has shaped and altered the course of small, independent publishing. In a mad dash through history, I offer students PowerPoint images of some of the wonderful contraptions that have helped shape printing in general, and small press publishing specifically—from ancient scrolls and Roman codexes; to 7th century Chinese wood block printing and Pi Sheng's 10th century moveable type; to 13th century Korean metal type moveable printing devices; to Chinese, Middle Eastern, and medieval papermaking; to Gutenberg's mid-15th century moveable type press; to Thomas Edison's monstrous Autographic Printing machine from the 1870s; to David Gestetner's 1880s Cyclostyle; to A.B. Dick's early hand-cranked mimeograph machines from the 1880s; to the first-ever xerographic image made by Chester Floyd Carlson of the Haloid Company of Rochester, New York, in 1938; to Haloid's eventual incarnation as the Xerox Corporation and the first high-speed Xerox office copier in 1958; to offset printers of the 1950s and 1960s; to ditto machines that sparked the "Mimeo Revolution" of the 1960s that spawned countless little magazines and small presses; and to current generation high-speed print-on-demand (POD) presses. What all these advancements and machines (and the technology that built them) have in common is that they revolutionized the mass production of written word texts, and by doing so created more accessibility to those printed texts to wider and diverse populations—and, more importantly for small publishers, created a democratization of publishing by decentralizing the centers of publishing power and control. Today, anyone with access to a half-decent computer installed with publishing programs such as PrintShop or InDesign can produce a magazine, chapbook, or full-length book that rivals mass market books in cost and, if done well, in looks. Similarly, this very-same technology allows for the decentralizing and democratization of publishing in the music world—how many CDs produced in someone's basement or garage using a home computer and recording software such as Reason or AcidPro and accompanied by jewelcase artwork, rival in sound and aesthetics, mass market CDs? In local book and music stores, basement-made CDs sit comfortably and competitively on the shelves next to CDs produced by Capitol, EMI, and other major labels.

One of the consequences of technology has been the proliferation of small presses and magazines (just as it allows for a proliferation of CDs and small, independent recording labels). One only has to contrast the first edition of founding editor Len Fulton's *The International Directory of Little Magazines & Small Presses* (Dustbooks) with the latest edition to see this proliferation: the forty-page first edition, published in 1965, listed two hundred fifty entries for magazines and small press publishers; the nearly eight-hundred page 2012-2013 48th edition, now available on CD-Rom, lists more than four thousand entries.

Several good histories of the small press and independent publishing movement in the United States are available for anyone wishing to explore its historical arc in more depth. The Council on Literary Magazines and Presses (CLMP), an invaluable organization and good friend to small press publishers, magazines, writers, and editors, hosts an excellent website: http://www.clmp.org/index.html, with links to bibliographies and essays about the history, influence, and role of small press and independent publishing in America, including Gayle Feldman's commissioned essay, "Independent Presses and 'Little' Magazines in American Culture: A Forty-Year Retrospective," and Charles B. Harris's "Independent Presses and the Future of Contemporary American Literature" from *Critique: Studies in Contemporary Fiction* 37.3 (Spring 1996). An excellent essay that illustrates how the proliferation of small magazines and publishers blossomed regionally is Gerald W. Haslam's, "Unknown Diversity: Small Presses and Little Magazines in the West, 1960-1980," an entry in *A Literary History of the American West* (Texas Christian Univ. Pr.,1987).

The scholarly literature about the significant role small, independent magazines, presses, and publishing has had in the shaping of American literature, especially in the 20th century, is abundant. And central to its story is the role technology has played in decentralizing and democratizing literature and writing, making it accessible to wider audiences, as well as providing a voice—through magazines and books—to marginalized and underrepresented populations. As we look to the future, inexpensive, accessible technology will continue (as we'll see later in the essay) to reshape and change the way we think about, create, distribute, market, and experience literature.

***

In 1975, during my first year of grad school, I met and soon became good friends with one of my professors who also shared a love for poetry. We soon discovered that we also shared the dream of starting a small poetry press some day, and after many talks, we did just that. I suspect many small press ventures begin this way. In 1978, in collaboration with two other friends, also grad students, we founded the first not-for-profit press in Indiana, applying for and then receiving our cherished 501(c)3 status. This allowed us to pay no federal income tax on sales of our nonprofit publishing activities, receive tax-deductible donations from individuals interested in supporting our efforts, and receive discounted postal rates. Mind you, we were permitted to make a profit from sales of the press, but because we were a not-for-profit press, we were not permitted to offer shares of stock for our company. Since we were not allowed to sell shares of stock, we had no shareholders to pay. But most of all, it allowed us to apply for state and federal grant monies to support the publishing of books. Over the next six to eight years, we published forty or so chapbooks and full-length collections of poetry, many of them by first-time Indiana authors, but also by more established writers from outside the state. Our press was pretty much a three- to four-person operation, including an artist-friend who did most of our design work. We also worked with a local printer who supported our venture with his printing expertise, patience, and sometimes in-kind contributions to the press when we were applying for grants.

During our early publishing years, we were awarded several small publishing grants from the Indiana Arts Commission and a large grant (large for us!) from the National Endowment for the Arts (NEA)—all supporting the publication of poetry. Our other main source of revenue, of course, was from book sales. Given our small size, we worked to get books in the hands of the authors who were the best promoters of their work. Most were great at promoting their work, which meant their books were selling and an audience was reading their poetry as well as learning about this new press in their home state. (To be clear, we are talking a few hundred copies of books—not thousands!)

I provide this personal backstory to introduce the next consideration: Government Funding. With 501(c)3 status, our press became eligible to apply for direct grant monies from the NEA, and indirectly from our state arts commission, since the NEA funnels monies to individual states for appropriation. According to its mission statement, the NEA "is a public agency dedicated to supporting excellence in the arts, both new and established; bringing the arts to all Americans; and providing leadership in arts education. Established by Congress in 1965 as an independent agency of the federal government, the Endowment is the nation's largest annual funder of the arts, bringing great art to all 50 states, including rural areas, inner cities, and military bases." If you are a National Public Radio listener, you've heard the NEA mantra: "A great nation deserves great art." The 1965 NEA budget totaled $2.9 million. The peak for the NEA budget occurred during the George Bush Sr., administration with a total of $175 million in 1992. President Obama's NEA budget request for fiscal year 2013-2014 was $154.255 million. Presidential hopeful Mitt Romney promised to eliminate funding of the NEA (as well as the National Endowment for the Humanities), as part of his austerity budget.

If you look at a pie chart of the 2012 federal budget of $3.7 trillion, notice how the pie is sliced. The largest slices go to defense (25 percent), health care (23 percent), and pensions (22 percent). Welfare gets 12 percent of the pie, and education 3 percent. A slice labeled "Other" gets 4 percent, and includes, among many, many other expenditures, the NEA. The NEA budget alone isn't a firm enough slice to stand alone on the plate—it would be more appropriate to represent the NEA budget as crumbs of the pie. The NEA for 2013 represents 0.004 percent of the federal budget. Compare this against the cost of war in Iraq for one day: $343 million (Department of Defense, 2007). During election years, you will often hear fiscally (and often socially) conservative politicians, eager to reduce the federal budget, list the NEA and the NEH among the first programs to be axed. Perhaps you recall Sarah Palin's remarks on FOX News's March 10, 2011, *Hannity* show: "NPR, National Endowment for the Arts, National Endowment for the Humanities, all those kind of frivolous things that government shouldn't be in the business of funding with tax dollars—those should all be on the chopping block as we talk about the $14-trillion debt that we're going to hand to our kids and our grandkids. Yes, those are the type of things that for more than one reason need to be cut." This makes for good sound bites, but does little to reduce the budget.

The 2007 report, *The Economic Impact of the Nonprofit Arts and Culture Industry in the Fargo-Moorhead Region*, sponsored by the Arts & Economic Prosperity III: Americans for the Arts, exposes the short-sightedness of such political trash talking. According to the report, there is

> compelling new evidence that the nonprofit arts and culture are a significant industry in the Fargo-Moorhead Region—one that generates $41.32 million in local economic activity. This spending—$17.35 million by nonprofit arts and culture organizations and an additional $23.97 million in event-related spending by their audiences—supports 1,386 full-time equivalent jobs, generates $26.37 million in household income to local residents, and delivers $4.92 million in local and state government revenue. This economic impact study sends a strong signal that when we support the arts, we not only enhance our quality of life, but we also invest in the Fargo-Moorhead Region's economic well-being.

Even if these "frivolous things," the NEA and NEH, were swept away like pie crumbs with the back of the hand, they barely would be noticed by the budget balancers. Who *would* notice their absence, however, would be the millions of Americans who, each year, participate in the arts—as performers, artists, readers, and audiences who attend local, regional, and national concerts, art exhibits, literary readings, plays, dances, and other arts programs supported and sponsored by the NEA. Next time you're waiting for the curtain to open or for the conductor to tap his wand against the music stand, search the program for the NEA logo to see if the frivolous event you are attending is being supported, in-part, by your tax dollars.

I raise the issue of government funding for the arts in order to ask a couple of important questions, questions that anyone about to start up a small press—and especially anyone applying for 501(c)3 status—should ask. The first is the larger question: Should the government be in the business of supporting the arts? The second, perhaps not as large as the first, but certainly as important: Does an artist—or editor, since we are talking specifically about publishing—in the pursuit of his or her art, give up or compromise any artistic freedom and integrity by entering into a relationship with the government? While these may seem more like philosophical or ethical considerations to contemplate, they do have very practical implications, as they may guide one's decision about government funding. For example, because public and private funding and granting agencies often drive their own social, political, and even aesthetic agendas, might a small press or magazine (or an individual artist) be inclined to alter its (or his or her) editorial or aesthetic vision to match (or at least not offend) that of the supporting agency in order to be more aligned with it, and thus more competitive, with the vision of the granting agency? Certainly government and private funding agencies have a right to set their own social, political, and aesthetic agendas, just as small presses and magazines and individual artists have the right to embrace their own social, political, and aesthetic agendas. Will differences of social, political, and aesthetic agendas enter into the equation when grant proposals are being read and monies handed out? Should an artist or publisher ever be beholden to the government?

***

Back in the early 1980s, soon after Ronald Reagan took office, our small, independent press in Indiana began to notice some different approaches to the way our not-for-profit organization was being asked to define itself. In order to apply for a grant, we now had to have an official financial audit completed by an independent auditor—if I recall, this was going to cost us about $300, a lot of money to us back then. We were also being asked to establish a board of directors for the press, as well as to consider hiring a development director, a fund-raiser, and a business manager.

We were being asked to look more like a small business than the three-or four-person operation that we were. I suspect accountability was driving some of these changes, along with a fiscal conservatism that was part of the Reagan Revolution. The small business model attempted to address fiscal responsibility, audience development, marketing, distribution, and fund-raising—certainly noteworthy goals for any not-for-profit organization. But this did not fit the vision that we had for ourselves or the press—we didn't want to become a small, independent press that modeled itself like a small business, at least the kind that was being proposed to us by the federal government. Not that there's anything wrong with that. It makes good sense, really, and many small, independent presses made successful transitions to the new model. But that isn't how we saw ourselves.

We were not interested in transforming ourselves into the kind of press that we were being asked to be. All the issues that the government wanted to address—marketing, distribution, fund-raising, audience development—are real and crucial issues for a successful press. But we didn't envision ourselves growing in this way. That is not the kind of organization and press we wanted to be. We were satisfied being a two- or three- or four-person press that published three or four books a year, with no office or storefront other than our garage and basement and our tabletops made with saw horses and abandoned doors and plywood. So we decided against continuing as a not-for-profit press and gave up the opportunities to apply for state or federal grants. We would tough it out by using our own money, money generated from sales, and money donated to the press by individuals who believed in our mission. There were other factors affecting our decision—I finished my degree, and in 1983 moved to Minnesota to begin my teaching career, removing me from the day-to-day operations with the press. We all had other full-time jobs. Also, bookstores, especially the big chains, were asking for larger discounts, didn't want to pay shipping costs, and their returns policies were not in the small publisher's best interest. During the intervening years since the mid-1980s, the press continued to publish chapbooks and a few full-length collections, but that was mostly done by my founding partner on his own time, at his own pace, and too often with his own money. We don't regret our decision not to grow the press into the small business model we were being asked to consider if we wanted to continue being eligible to apply for state or federal grant monies. We didn't think of our decision as taking a great moral or ethical stance against Goliath Government. Rather, we just wanted to continue along, publishing a few books of poetry a year, the way we originally had envisioned ourselves doing.

***

It is easy to find work to publish. And these days, with e-publishing, it is easier than ever to publish that work. The more difficult task—as I think it has always been—is marketing, distributing, and selling those books once they are published. I have a hunch that there are garages, storage rooms, and basements all over the United States filled with cartons of books that were printed with the support of private, state, or federal grant monies, from the pre-print-on-demand era, when low cost per unit prices tempted overly optimistic small press editors and publishers to print two thousand copies of a book of poems instead of five hundred copies. Print-on-demand publishing has all but eliminated over-production and costly inventory and warehousing costs for small publishers. In the world of poetry, where two thousand copies of a book of poems sold over a five-year period is considered a successful title, there are more books than ever before being published. Thanks to technology, much has happened in the publishing world in the past thirty years to make marketing and distribution much easier now than it was in the late 1970s and early 1980s. From my reading of *The Bowker Library and Trade Almanac*, a standard of the book industry, I discovered that in 1980, 779 new books, editions, and mass-market paperbacks of poetry and drama were published. In 2010, the number of new books of poetry and drama published leaped to 11,405! And these figures don't account for digital-only publications. The new technology and the relative ease of accessibility to it have resulted in a marketplace that's more competitive than ever before.

Additionally, the new players on the block—self-publishing and print-on-demand services such as AuthorSolutions (now owned by Penguin's parent company, Pearson), BiblioBazaar, iUniverse, Xlibris, AuthorHouse, LuLu Enterprises, Smashwords, and CreateSpace—have changed the game. Contracting for their author and publishing services (you can spend as little or as much money as you want acquiring their levels of service), and offering a do-it-yourself process, you can print (hard copy or digital), publicize, market, and distribute your book and simply bypass the traditional route to publication. Little, if any, editorial judgment is made about the quality of the manuscript. If you have the money, you can publish your book. As satisfied AuthorHouse customers Andy and Bernice Tate, authors of four AuthorHouse children's books, state on the AuthorHouse website, "You can go to the website and they will tell you everything you need to know, and a whole bunch of stuff you didn't know you needed to know. That's what we found out." Today, self-publishing and print-on-demand services have turned publishing into a one-stop shopping adventure. The following report from the 2011 *Bowker Annual Book Production Report* reflects the growing impact e-book publishing is having on traditional publishing:

> Bowker, the global leader in bibliographic information, released its annual report on U.S. print book publishing, compiled from its Books In Print® database. Based on preliminary figures from U.S. publishers, Bowker [projected] that despite the popularity of e-books, traditional U.S. print title output in 2010 increased 5%. Output of new titles and editions increased from 302,410 in 2009 to a projected 316,480 in 2010. The 5% increase comes on the heels of a 4% increase the previous year based on the final 2008-2009 figures.

The non-traditional sector continues its explosive growth, increasing 169 percent from 1,033,065 in 2009 to an amazing 2,776,260 in 2010. These books, marketed almost exclusively on the web, are largely on-demand titles produced by reprint houses specializing in public domain works and by presses catering to self-publishers and "micro-niche" publications. "These publication figures from both traditional and non-traditional publishers confirm that print production is alive and well, and can still be supported in this highly dynamic marketplace," said Kelly Gallagher, vice president of publishing services for Bowker. "Especially on the non-traditional side, we're seeing the reprint business's internet-driven business model expand dramatically. It will be interesting to see in the coming years how well it succeeds in the long-term.

Non-traditional print-on-demand is concentrated in a handful of houses. In 2008, the production of non-traditional print-on-demand books surpassed traditional book publishing for the first time and since then, its growth has been staggering. Now almost eight times the output of traditional titles, the market is dominated by a handful of publishers. In fact, the top three publishers accounted for nearly 87 percent of total titles produced in 2010. E-publishers and e-publishing have changed the way books can be acquired, produced, marketed, and distributed. I don't think they are going away, as the technology becomes more sophisticated in the future.

The challenge for any publisher (or author) is a basic one: How do you get books into the hands of readers. For small, independent presses, author readings have been among the best ways to market a title. Most first-time and emerging authors are eager and willing promoters of their books, and anything the publisher can do to help make that happen is worth their while. Most small presses cannot afford to send their authors on the traditional promotional reading tour of bookstores, or purchase costly display ads in industry journals and literary magazines. They rely, for the most part, on word-of-mouth promotion by readers, author readings, targeted mailings, and book reviews—when they can get them. More often, the author, in concert with the publisher, works to arrange readings at bookstores, college campuses, coffee houses, libraries, art galleries, and other literary-friendly venues. By putting books directly into the hands of an author—either by consignment or by offering deep author discounts—the author can sell books at his or her readings, eliminating multiple expensive shipping costs, and guarantee that the books will be at the reading venue when the author arrives.

But once again, technology offers alternatives to traditional marketing. The rise of social media is changing this, too. Social media is a relatively low-cost option for small presses who cannot compete in the world of costly print ads, and a small press editor or publisher with average tech savvy can roll out an attractive, direct ad campaign for a book (or for the press, itself), using a combination of social media such as Facebook, Twitter, MySpace, Youtube, Tumblr, blogs, vlogs, internet forums, weblogs, podcasts, and dozens of other options.

Getting books into the marketplace always has been the biggest challenge faced by small press publishers. While local and (sometimes regional) bookstores often are willing to stock titles by local authors and small presses, getting books into larger, more geographically diverse markets is another matter. As long as I have been involved with small press publishing, marketing and distribution have been perennial topics of conversations whenever two or more small press editors gather at book fairs. To deal with this challenge, distribution cooperatives such as Small Press Distribution and Consortium Book Sales and Distribution emerged from earlier incarnations from the 1970s and 1980s. Consortium (whose services are used by New Rivers Press),

> grew out of a small book wholesaling cooperative in 1985 to become a full-service distributor, and we quickly earned a reputation as an advocate for independent publishers. As our reputation and expertise grew, so did our publisher base. We now represent more than 90 independent publishers from the United States, Canada, Europe, India, and Australia, enabling them to successfully reach the trade, library, and academic audiences for their books. We understand the importance of ideas, and our goal as a distributor is to introduce those ideas—some that may otherwise not be heard—to the world. Through an award-winning literary tradition, Consortium has fostered innovation and excellence in publishing—our publishers' authors are among the most distinguished and honored in the publishing community. We offer an incredibly diverse range of books, including fiction, poetry, gay and lesbian studies, politics, music, art, history, and children's books, just to name a few. To our customers, Consortium represents a source for books of quality and distinction. (http://www.cbsd.com/about.aspx)

One of the oldest small press distributors in the United States, Small Press Distribution of Berkeley, California,

> was founded in 1969 by Peter Howard of Serendipity Books and Jack Shoemaker of Sand Dollar Press. The fledgling or-

ganization provided small-scale distribution services for only five publishers. Initially called Serendipity Books Distribution, it was renamed Small Press Distribution by the late 1970s. Throughout the 1970s and 1980s, the organization periodically assembled the new titles of their publishers into printed catalogs, thus providing a vital link to underground literature for writers and readers around the US. By 1980, SPD was distributing the books of about 40 small publishers; by 1990, the number had grown to 330. Today, SPD distributes books for approximately 400 publishers, each of whom produces anywhere from one to twenty books a year.

SPD became an official 501(c)3 non-profit in 1996. Since that time, its sales and staff have grown despite the demise of many independent bookstores that previously operated as its most consistent customer base. Given the nature of commercial publishing and for-profit book distribution, a case can be made that SPD has played a vital role in keeping grassroots, noncommercial poetry and fiction continuously available in the U.S. to new generations of readers over the last three decades. (http://en.wikipedia.org/wiki/Small_Press_Distribution)

Another player in the distribution game is Chicago Distribution Center (CDC) of the University of Chicago Press. The CDC serves as a distribution "hub" for dozens of academic presses (many of them non-for-profit), and allows the presses to outsource services they once provided themselves, but that now have become too costly to continue. The CDC Services Page states:

Two hundred seventy-three thousand square feet. Nearly twelve million books in inventory. Over fifty thousand active ISBNs. More than nineteen thousand units shipped daily. Welcome to the Chicago Distribution Center. CDC receives, picks, packs, and ships orders for the University of Chicago Press's Books and Journals Divisions. What really makes its services impressive, however, is that it also functions as the hub for more than fifty scholarly publishers. Since 1991, CDC has provided many of the world's finest academic publishers with state-of-the-art fulfillment, customer service, collection, and reporting. (http://www.press.uchicago.edu/cdc.html)

If you read the back pages of university press catalogs, you will see a list of names of book representatives who cover various United States regions and foreign markets. For small press editors, hiring book representatives to promote their titles to booksellers across the United States and abroad is an impossibility—thus, the utility, efficiency, and convenience of contracting with SPD, Consortium (acquired by Perseus Books Group in 2006), or the Chicago Distribution Center. However, it is not without some cost to the small press to access the distribution, sales, and marketing services offered by these professional book distributors.

The November 26, 2007, cover of *Newsweek* magazine boldly proclaims: "Books Aren't Dead. They're Just Going Digital." Holding up an Amazon Kindle, face half-hidden behind it, is the smiling face of Jeff Bezos, founder and CEO of Amazon.com, Inc. Six years later, estimates of e-reader devices in the United States alone range from 40 million to 60 million, including the various generations of Kindles, Nooks, Sony and Kobo Vox e-readers, Blios, and other less popular variations of electronic reading devices. According to Michael Mace of Rubicon Consulting, "The most-used device for reading an eBook is a personal computer (47 percent); Amazon Kindle is number two (32 percent), followed by Apple's iPhone and iPod Touch (21 percent)." E-reader devices have become popular Christmas gift items, especially among people who, otherwise, would not think of giving a book for a Christmas gift. BBC News reports that, "in January 2011, online retailer Amazon.com reported that it sold three times as many Kindle books as hardcover books. As of that same month, the company also began selling more Kindle books than paperbacks" (http://www.bbc.co.uk/news/business-12305015).

The Association of American Presses reports that e-book sales in the United States nearly tripled between January and October 2009 ($127.3 million) and January and October 2010 ($345.3 million). In 2011, e-books outsold hardcover books for the first time. Self-published titles have nearly tripled, growing 287 percent since 2006. A recent trend in book buying (and other product buying as well) known as "showrooming" has cut into the sales of hardcover and paperback books. Showrooming is the practice of examining merchandise in a retail store and then returning home to research the web for the same product but for a lower cost and then make an online purchase. A book buyer, for example, might go to Barnes and Noble, find and preview a book by flipping through it (perhaps while sipping a latte at the in-store Starbucks) then return home, look for a less-expensive online edition, and either purchase the same book or download it to his or her e-reader. Many retailers are experiencing a form of showrooming, as cost-conscious consumers, with easy access to the technology, have become savvy shoppers.

***

I always wrap-up my presentation to the Intro to Publishing class with a discussion of the future of the book. Students are creative thinkers when I ask them to imagine how the book and book publishing will look in ten and twenty-five years. While I hesitate to predict the future of the book and book publishing, I do suggest to them that the future will look nothing like the present. John B. Thompson, author of *Merchants of Culture: The Publishing Business in the Twenty-First Century* (Polity, 2010), writes that, "The digital revolution may be a revolution of the *process* of publishing—production and printing, sales and marketing, inventory control and distribution—but the product has pretty much stayed the same."

The considerations that I discuss with the students—technology; government funding for the arts; business models for operating a small, independent publishing company; and marketing and distribution of books—surely will continue to play a role in that future. I conclude my presentation to the Intro to Publishing class with a short YouTube video, which demonstrates an EBM, an Espresso Book Machine, in action. According to the EBM website:

> The patented Espresso Book Machine® (EBM) makes a paperback book in minutes, at point of need. Through its EspressNet® digital catalog of content, books can be ordered online or onsite at bookstores, libraries, and non-bookstore retailers. Over seven million in-copyright and public-domain titles are available on the network. The technology is also ideal for self and custom publishing. (http://ondemandbooks.com/ebm_overview.php)

Coincidentally, the last time I gave the presentation, the book being printed in the YouTube demo video was the very same textbook the students were reading for their Intro to Publishing class! While the EBM hasn't found its way to MSUM's campus yet, a few transfer students shared their EBM experiences of buying textbooks for their courses at their previous universities. The cost for an EBM machine is around $150,000, but there's a model that's being developed for purchase for about $90,000. I suspect universities will rent EBMs (and acquire the service agreement, as they now do with high-speed photocopiers) rather than purchase them. Perhaps campus bookstores of the future will look more like quick-print shops, convenience stores, or vending arcades more than they will look like bookstores.

Before I open up the class for a Q&A session, I suggest that anyone interested in entering the world of small, independent publishing (or larger for-profit publishing, for that matter) needs to be knowledgeable about developing technology and trends that are changing the nature of the business on a daily basis. In addition to taking their required courses in publishing and writing, I advise them to take courses in art, graphic design, typography and book design, public relations and marketing, as well as courses in entrepreneurship, non-profit organizations, and running small businesses. Lastly, I remind them that, for the most part, people don't get into the small, independent publishing business because of their love and passion for small, independent press publishing—rather, they become involved with small, independent publishing because of their love and passion for literature—poetry, fiction, all and any forms of the written word.

For Further Reading

Using key word searches (small presses, small press history, independent publishing, self-publishing, small press in United States), you will be directed to the plethora of information about small, independent publishers, and publishing out there on the Internet. Below I've listed some resources that I have found helpful. Some pre-date the digital revolution, but they highlight the historical challenges that the small, independent editor and publisher have faced. The histories of small magazines and small presses is intertwined, as many small presses were offshoots of small magazines.

Abel, Richard E. and Lyman W. Newman, eds. *Scholarly Publishing: Books, Journals, Publishers and Libraries in the Twentieth Century*. Hoboken: Wiley, 2002.

Anderson, Elliott, and Mary Kinzie, eds. *The Little Magazine in America: A Modern Documentary History*. Yonkers: Pushcart, 1978.

Bowker Online. www.bowker.com

Bruchac, Joseph. *How to Start and Sustain a Literary Magazine*. Austin: Provision House, 1980.

Chielens, Edward E., ed. *American Literary Magazines: The Twentieth Century*. Westport: Greenwood Press, 1992.

Clay, Steve and Rodney Phillips. "A Little History of the Mimeograph Revolution." *GraneryBooks*. http://www.granarybooks.com/books/clay/clay4.html.

Council of Literary Magazines and Small Presses.

Dennison, Sally. *[Alternative] Literary Publishing: Five Modern Histories*. Iowa City: University of Iowa Press, 1986.

Epstein, Jason. *Book Business: Publishing: Past, Present, and Future*. New York: W. W. Norton & Co., 2000. 2002 Reprint.

Feldman, Gayle, "Independent Presses and 'Little' Magazines in American Culture: A Forty-Year Retrospective," *Clmp.org*. https://www.clmp.org/indie_publishing/feldman.html.

Gabriel, Michael R. "The Astonishing Growth of Small Publishers." *Journal of Popular Culture 24* (1990): 61–68.

Givler, Peter. "University Press Publishing in the United States." *AAUP*. http://www.aaupnet.org/about-aaup/about-university-presses/history-of-university-presses.

Henderson, Bill, ed. *The Art of Literary Publishing: Editors on Their Craft*. Wainscott: Pushcart Press, 1980.

Henderson, Bill, ed. *The Publish It Yourself Handbook: Literary Tradition & How-To*. Wainscott: Pushcart Press, 1998.

Hoffman, Frederick J., Charles Allen, and Carolyn F. Ulrich. *The Little Magazine: A History and Bibliography*. Princeton: Princeton University Press, 1946.

Kruchow, Diane and Curt Johnson. *Green Isle in the Sea: An Informal History of the Alternative Press, 1960-85*. Highland Park: December Press, 1986.

Laughing Bear Newsletter. www.laughingbear.com.

The Library and Book Trade Almanac (formerly The Bowker Annual).

McLaughlin, Robert L. "Oppositional Aesthetics/Oppositional Ideologies: A Brief Cultural History of Alternative Publishing in the U.S." *LitLine*. http://litline.org/mclaughlin.html.

O'Donnell, Kevin, Jr. "How Thor Power Hammered Publishing." *Science Fiction Writers of America*. http://www.sfwa.org.

Person, Tom. "The Surviving Small Press: The Role of Literary Publishing." *Laughing Bear Newsletter #118*, 2000. http://www.laughingbear.com.

Scott, Debra Leigh. "Small Presses & Literary Magazines Continue To Innovate & Thrive." *New York Journal of Books*. 10 April 2011. http://cliffordgarstang.com.

SelfPublishedAuthor. (Bowker).

Small Press Center for Independent Publishing.

Staley, Eric. "Influence, Commerce, and the Literary Magazine." *Missouri Review 7*. Fall 1983. 177–93.

Thompson, John B. *Merchants of Culture: The Publishing Business in the Twenty-First Century*. Polity: 2010.

Von Hallberg, Robert. *American Poetry and Culture, 1945–1980*. Cambridge: Harvard UP, 1985.

SUZZANNE KELLEY

Suzzanne Kelley started working with New Rivers Press in October of 2009. Her background in publishing, education, and working with nonprofits makes for a good fit for the activities of a nonprofit literary teaching press.

89823

Shaking out dozens of pages, I share with my class the long list of ISBNs (International Standard Book Numbers) that Bill Truesdale bought who-knows-how-many years ago. Each page, still attached to the one previous with perforated tear lines and holes in a strip along each side for an old-fashioned tractor-fed printer, is yellowed with age and cigarette smoke. Hand-written notations identify the author's name and book title for each work assigned an ISBN, nearing four hundred now in number, but with a thousand more as-yet-unassigned ISBNs to go.

Each ISBN has one series of numbers in common: 89823. This five-digit code, embedded in the thirteen-digit number, identifies a book as belonging to New Rivers Press. Only New Rivers Press books can carry this unique series of digits. My Introduction to Publishing class and I marvel at our imagined image of Truesdale, sitting forward in his chair, elbows on his desk, one hand propping up his chin while his other hand holds a cigarette, gazing through his black-rimmed glasses to witness the printing of this scroll, watching each page land in a self-folding pile at the end of a table, and all the while envisioning the names of books to be penciled in after each line in their turn. It is an imagining that grounds us in the past and the present of New Rivers Press.

My students often ask what route a person takes to become an editor. Truesdale's path came about from his experience as a writer and a poet, and from his frustration for new authors to get their work in print. He began his publishing career in a dusty, abandoned shed as a way to help other writers circumvent that frustration. My own entry to publishing came from the receiving end of publishers, from being an avid reader at an early age, devouring books as fast as I could get them from our little library in Fairbanks, Alaska. A quiet log cabin located alongside the Chena River, our public library was a warren of rooms with books, poor lighting except for that which came in through the windows to illuminate the dust motes and the story titles on the book spines. In one secluded corner was a plush but worn and faded chair, where I could sample the first paragraphs of an Agatha Christie mystery or begin a new adventure with Nancy Drew. My library card, with its engraved-number slip of metal embedded in thick cardboard—long before plastic cards with barcodes—entitled me to check out a small stack of books, a treasure trove for an eight-year-old who lived out in the country in yet another log cabin, with lots of wintry dark hours to fill with words about places and times and adventures. I've not found a common route to recommend to my students who seek employment in the publishing industry except that they, like Truesdale and I, must have a love for story, poetry, books.

I've worked at a number of jobs that have, unbeknownst to me at the time, honed the skills needed to work as a managing editor and an educator in publishing. My typing skills landed me jobs with the NASA Tracking Station (as a secretary in Facilities) and then with the Alaska State Troopers Civil Section (as an assistant to the Warrants Clerk). For eight years I worked as the director of a nonprofit public library—a very small one in a small Texas town where I was the story lady, the program coordinator, the grant writer, the records manager, the circulation clerk, and, since there wasn't a public bathroom, I was even the keeper of the porta-potty. While those were good and interesting jobs, I wanted to go on to college, which I did as a non-traditional—otherwise known as older-than-average—student with two elementary-school-age sons. I eventually graduated from the University of Texas at Austin with a teaching degree and a minor in history. I taught reading, writing, and social studies to fifth-graders at a little Texas school appropriately named Shady Grove Elementary.

I would probably be retiring today from my public school teaching days, but in 2000, I had the good fortune to win a National Endowment for the Humanities (NEH) scholarship. My letters of recommendation from administrators and peers, my several years of teaching experience, and my essay about being ten years old and riding with siblings and parents from Alaska to Wyoming in a metallic blue Pontiac in 1967, garnered me a place with fourteen other teachers who wanted to learn about history and memory in the Great Plains from Texas to Saskatchewan. I believe it was my telling of wandering through a Wyoming wheat field, the wheat heads tickling the undersides of my arms stretched out wide, and my first time to see sky and field meeting at the horizon without the interruption of Alaska mountain ranges, that won my seat in the humanities seminar.

My NEH experience—five weeks spent reading and writing and talking about what we read and wrote—changed my life forever. I had finally found a circle of odd fellows who, like me, had books on the brain. With my children grown and on their own scholastic endeavors, I returned to college, earning first a master's in history from the University of Central Oklahoma and then a doctorate from North Dakota State University. All of my graduate studies were anchored in internship experiences in publishing with *The Chronicles of Oklahoma*, *The American Review of China Studies*, and *Oklahoma Politics*, followed by a fellowship where I was appointed managing editor of *Agricultural History* (an international journal) and then book editor for the North Dakota Institute for Regional Studies Press.

My PhD program required that I study two foreign languages. I had one requirement completed—college credits in Spanish—but I needed to fulfill the second before graduation. I successfully made the argument that I might be allowed to substitute for a second language the twelve credits required for a graduate-level Certificate in Publishing at Minnesota State University Moorhead. Under the direction of Donna Carlson, I completed the certificate in 2007 in the still fairly-new program in publishing, one of less than a handful in the nation at that time.

In the fall of 2009, I was serving as Preservation North Dakota's president and working as a for-hire historian in far-north Warroad, Minnesota, collecting photos and documents to determine if St. Mary's, the largest log church in the world, was eligible for the National Register of Historic Places. Out of the blue, Carlson called, and despite poor cell phone reception in the field, I heard her say she was retiring and moving to Connecticut. She asked if I would care to apply for her job. I wasted no time in getting myself to Minnesota State University Moorhead (MSUM) and an interview with Senior Editor Alan Davis and Director Wayne Gudmundson.

My organizational abilities and teaching skills, my experience with nonprofit organizations and publishing entities—along with my Certificate in Publishing—helped me to navigate my way through the various duties of my job as managing editor (and co-director since Wayne Gudmundson's retirement) for New Rivers Press. Carlson taught me the cycles of New Rivers Press operations, which run in accord as much as possible with the academic cycles of MSUM. The managing editor's job for New Rivers Press encompasses a variety of responsibilities that elsewhere would belong to multiple employees. Alan Davis, as senior editor, is in charge of acquisitions and substantive editing. That may not sound too taxing and more like fun, but he reviews nearly one thousand manuscripts a year, he actively seeks submissions, and he has to make those tough decisions that narrow the choices down to three or more book-length manuscripts that, when combined with our competition manuscripts, will become our frontlist. He is also the go-to guy for delicate negotiations and diplomacy (yes, they are required), as I am often too quick to reply when my ire is raised. Once the manuscripts are acquired, it is my job to take them through all the stages of production and to manage the day-to-day operations of the press, including:

- collecting contracts, author questionnaires, photos, and permissions from our authors;
- reading the acquired manuscripts and then obtaining copies for book teams to work with;
- mentoring book teams at every stage of their work and overseeing their relationships with authors and designers;
- teaching the Introduction to Publishing and Practicum in Publishing courses (which requires staying up-to-date with the literature and practice of the field);
- planning and conducting a day-long (from 6:30 a.m. until midnight) tour to Minneapolis-St. Paul for twenty to forty students to various publishing-related sites, which have included BookMobile, Coffee House Press, Milkweed Editions, the Loft Literary Center, Minnesota Center for Book Arts, Capstone, and Common Good Books;
- guiding first-time authors through the publication and marketing processes;
- working with the MFA program (until recently, when it ended) and independent study graduate students, interns (graduate and undergraduate), and honors apprentices, and supervising volunteers and non-resident students;
- negotiating final edits and cover designs with our art director, Allen Sheets, designers, and authors;
- conducting fund-raising events, writing grant applications, and administering grants;
- keeping track of financing and expenditures for events, competitions, book production, marketing and publicity, and book distribution;
- advertising and overseeing our various submissions periods: general (May), American Fiction Short Story Award (February 1 to June 15), Electronic Book Series (July 1 to September 1), Many Voices Project (September 15 to November 1);

• re-reading each manuscript after the book teams, sending the manuscripts to the designers, re-reading the manuscripts after the designers, sending the designed interiors to the authors to check for errors, re-reading manuscripts after errors have been corrected, sending the interior designs to BookMobile (our printer of choice) to obtain advance review copies, proofreading the advance review copies and sending them out across the United States for review, overseeing any corrections yet to be made, proofreading the corrected version for BookMobile to print, distributing the books to Consortium Books Sales & Distribution, to authors, and to our on-site inventory space, and then re-reading books converted to electronic versions;
• managing all of our social network communications;
• and working to design and implement new program initiatives such as our Electronic Book Series and converting our backlist to e-books.

As I noted earlier, with larger press organizations, there would be multiple employees to take on all of these tasks, but the day-to-day operations I've just described are typical—except for the teaching and mentoring and multiple-reading parts—for small, nonprofit presses everywhere with one or two people carrying the load. No matter how tired I might feel at the end of day, I know that there are dozens of other small press managing editors who tote manuscripts and grant applications home to read after hours.

While the workload is typical of a small press operation, New Rivers Press is atypical in that in the early part of this decade, it transitioned to a teaching press. At the time, such an enterprise was a curiosity, and while other institutions have since incorporated publishing fields of study into their programs, we are the *only* one that gives a well-rounded, hands-on, real product experience of exceptional magnitude. In fact, as Katie Hansen (one of our long-term honors apprentices) jubilantly exclaimed to someone visiting our office, "The students get to do *all* the work!"

I confess to being taken aback by Katie's remark, as I was pretty sure that I was clocking in a lot of hours, but I stopped myself from correcting her, for it is just that sense of ownership and pride, based on real responsibility and experience, that I work to cultivate. Students have a hand in nearly every aspect of our operations: logging in submissions, planning and implementing events, designing book covers and interiors, editing manuscripts and creating marketing materials, attending conferences and manning exhibit booths, and even, most recently, developing a crowdfunding campaign on Indiegogo to assist with the production of *Paper Camera*.

Introduction to Publishing students depart from MSUM at 6:30 a.m. for an all-day tour of publishing sites in the Twin Cities.

Many times I have been asked if it wouldn't be faster and more efficient just to do these things myself. The answer is yes, perhaps, but New Rivers Press would not be nearly as fun to work for and we would not come up with nearly the number of clever ideas. The broad base of knowledge and expertise that the students and interns contribute help us to be that much more professional in the content and delivery of our books. And, I have learned much from my students (working with Excel and Twitter come immediately to mind, so thank you Emilee Ruhland!), making the trade-off of information immeasurably valuable. The success of the program lies in the craft of its early design, and so kudos and all my admiration go to Wayne Gudmundson, Alan Davis, and Donna Carlson.

Our students elect to work with New Rivers Press for a variety of reasons. Some students aspire to be published authors, or to work in some aspect of publishing. During one class period we came up with some twenty-seven different jobs in publishing, including acting as agent, accounting, designing, and, of course—the only thing they all thought they would be doing when they entered the course: editing, and what none thought they would be doing: creating book trailers.

Working within a university has its advantages and disadvantages. We benefit by the fresh energy and ideas of our students, we have a superb location (with windows!) in the oldest historic building on campus, access to up-to-date technology, and great storage space for our on-site inventory. On occasion we can call on some of the grounds crew for heavy-lifting duty. The drawbacks, however, can be a challenge and should be mentioned.

When New Rivers Press came to Minnesota State University Moorhead, we had to give up our nonprofit 501(c)3 status. We still operate with nonprofit 501(c)3 status under the Alumni Foundation and with the university's government nonprofit status, but Minnesota's attorney general determined that we had to dissolve our own nonprofit status. In 1982 New Rivers Press became one of the first nonprofit literary presses to obtain a 501(c)3 designation, a historical feat accomplished by Truesdale; it is a shame to have had to relinquish that designation for "one of the oldest continuously publishing literary presses in the country," as New Rivers Press was described by books editor Mary Ann Grossmann in the *Pioneer Press* (April 12, 2001).

While we can raise funds under the university's umbrella, the university does not allocate line-item funding for our operations. Davis receives some faculty release time from instructional duties, as does poetry professor in the MSUM English department, Kevin Carollo, who receives a smaller portion for his work in coordinating the poetry section of our Many Voices Project, and I receive adjunct salary for teaching the two courses. Our space and equipment are free to us. All operations requiring cash—paying for supplies, printing, shipping, marketing, publicity, the managing editor's salary, and more— however, must be raised by New Rivers Press through grants, sales, individual donations, and (as a bone of contention among purists) reading fees for our competitions. Our most generous line of support for decades has come from The McKnight Foundation, which funded publications during Truesdale's management, paid the press's debt so that the transfer could be made to MSUM after Truesdale's passing, and continues today with much-needed funds for operational support. Additional support has come our way recently from the Dawson Family Fund (which secured an endowment fund for New Rivers Press), Lake Region Arts Council, the North Dakota Ethics Institute, and Northern Lights Library Network. All of these resources allow us to pay honorariums for prizewinners and judges and to keep our day-to-day operations afloat. The combination of efforts and resources has made it possible for New Rivers Press to continue its traditions of publishing new, emerging, and established authors of contemporary literature while offering learning opportunities.

The last challenge I'll mention is the bureaucracy of working within a university institution. Taking action on almost any matter is slowed down by having to obtain permissions and multiple signatures and by having to explain and justify anew just *why* we operate the way we do. For instance, these questions come up frequently: Why must you keep all of your backlist titles? Why don't you just get rid of all those books and do away with all of your inventory problems? The problems include price per square foot for floor space on campus, monthly rent fees for keeping stock with our distributor (although we have decreased that cost to a minimum by removing excess books to our own location), and the potentially hefty cost of moving inventory from one distributor to another. Indeed, our most recent and nerve-wracking hold-up came when it was time to reassess our contract with our distributor, Consortium Book Sales & Distribution (CBSD).

When New Rivers Press came to MSUM, CBSD was already in place as our distributor, and the negotiations to bring the press to MSUM included the condition that we continue to contract with CBSD for distribution services for at least five years. Now, nearly eleven years later, CBSD has determined to revisit the terms of our contract. For the past decade we have published only in the fall season, which creates sort of a boom and bust scenario with our distributor. For part of the year, when sales are great, we carry a positive balance with CBSD and we even get paid after distribution expenses are deducted. However, we carry a negative balance, generally ranging from $2000 to $4000, when returns come in from booksellers, catalog charges mount, and other monthly charges accrue. In our earlier days, that was not too big a problem, because the negative balance was more than made up for when sales rolled in again following our new publications; CBSD simply carried any negative balance over to the next period of prosperity. During the past decade CBSD moved its distribution hub from Minneapolis to Jackson, Tennessee, when CBSD was acquired by the larger Perseus Distribution company. The new terms now required by CBSD include publishing in multiple seasons (a difficulty for us as we must also accommodate the academic cycle) and accepting a larger deduction in our sales checks to be held in reserve against possible negative balances. Renegotiating contracts such as one with our distributor is not something we are allowed to handle in-house; we must go through several channels within the university system with experts who know much about contracts but not so much about the business of publishing.

***

As an editor and historian, I have read with relish some of the New Rivers Press and C.W. Truesdale documents now housed at the University of Minnesota Libraries. I am learning, albeit more slowly than I wish, about New Rivers Press's past. It was that curiosity along with the advent of anniversary celebrations that led to the development of *Paper Camera*. My admiration for Bill Truesdale has only grown through this process, even though by many accounts he could be difficult. I wish we could have met. It would be interesting to hear his thoughts on where the press is today.

The move from the Twin Cities and its lively literary scene was cause for much discussion; wary eyes followed our transition, wondering if the press would founder or, perhaps worse, become a venue for faculty to have a straight shot at publication and leave the new and emerging authors at large at a loss. Lisa Bullard, New Rivers Press's interim director in 2001, helped smooth the way. In the July/August 2001 issue of *Poets & Writers*, Bullard noted that "Bill Truesdale, who founded the press and who was the leader for thirty years, started in an academic setting." She referred perhaps to his years as a member of the faculty at the private liberal arts college, Macalester, located in St. Paul, Minnesota. "In a way," Bullard continued, "having New Rivers on a campus is a nice return to the origins."

In the previous issue of *Poets & Writers* (May/June 2001), the headline "New Rivers Press Suffers Great Loss" announced that in January "the oldest literary nonprofit publisher in Minnesota," New Rivers Press, had begun proceedings for suspending operations and that on February 26 Truesdale had died after his "long battle with heart disease." He was seventy-one years old. His press was thirty-two, and he had published more than three hundred books. Citing Truesdale's obituary, the article states that "[i]n 1978 [Truesdale] came to the Twin Cities and, alongside other nonprofit publishing mavericks such as Milkweed Edition's Emilie Buchwald and Coffee House Press's Allan Kornblum, made a writers' destination out of what once had been literary flyoverland."

Truesdale's death was not the only devastation to cause New Rivers Press to suffer. High rates of returns from the big chain bookstores led to the press's inability to keep up payments on its line of credit, and the simultaneous terminal illness of Phyllis Jendro, New Rivers Press's executive director, put the press in dire straits. Bullard and the board of directors were forced to cut staff, including marketing staff, leaving just four people. Bullard still held a positive view, however, and in the May/June article noted that "the board of directors is cautiously optimistic about setting up a partnership, but is willing to wait for 'a committed, stable partner'" before fully considering the option of closing for good. While another Twin Cities press and a local literary organization expressed interest in becoming that partner, it was Minnesota State University Moorhead that won the day.

New Rivers Press, in partnership with MSUM, continues to transition and grow and, most importantly, to publish new and emerging authors. Every spring when I take my Introduction to Publishing students to the Twin Cities, I see that we are holding our own, even away from Minnesota's literary center, publishing authors who become finalists and/or win awards in state, regional, and national competitions. We keep alive the literary publishing traditions that Truesdale initiated and make it possible for students—potential authors and publishers themselves—to learn about this fast-changing industry. As my students and I study together the handwritten entries made by Truesdale and now Davis on the long scroll of ISBNs, we comprehend the impact New Rivers Press has had on the corpus of literary works. We view the empty lines, yet to be filled, and we wonder together about the works to come.

The Pattern

The mountains had one
and the ocean waves had another.

There was one in the clouds
and in a bird's feathers.

From the beginning, something
was established; it had its own

language and customs—it was
called by our two names.

After a while, there was nothing
we could do about it.

Clint McCown has a long history with New Rivers Press, serving as judge for our American Fiction Prize and twice winning the prize prior to that. In 2012 New Rivers Press published his novel, Haints, *which won first place for literary novels in the Midwest Independent Publishers Award.*

Curves and Angles

*T*he universe is a battleground between curves and angles. The world is round, its movement circular, but most of its makeup is sharp-edged, from the sheer cliff faces of Everest to the smallest grains of sand. We build our lives between these two extremes, and marry the two geometries in myriad ways.

The sweeping curve of the clock hand is powered by the interlocking angles of its gears.

The angles of a kite keep it streaming through the ongoing curve of the wind.

Every ball game is played on a field of straight lines and calculated angles.

Look at numbers: A zero is a perfect self-completing curve, while the following integer, 1, is the straight and primary building block of every angle. The number 4 is all angles, but double that and 8 is all curves.

The alphabet, likewise, is where we fit curves to angles to create contrasting shapes, and from those shapes we have fashioned a form of communication. Contrasting shapes have always been at the heart of communication, whether we're talking about cuneiform tablets, the dots and dashes of Morse code, or the 0-1 alternations of binary computer programming.

But what does any of this have to do with New Rivers Press? The answer to that depends, I suppose, on how you look at things. I might be veering sharply away from one subject to another, making New Rivers an angular departure from my previous direction. Or maybe I've been working a curve all along, bending toward this topic from the very beginning. Either way, New Rivers Press is a contrasting shape, when looked at against the backdrop of the traditional publishing industry. It's a new combination of curves and angles; a new form of communication.

How did Michelangelo work on his sculptures? With a sharp-edged chisel. And every piece of stone he chipped away was itself sharp-edged, a tiny blade of stone. Yet his results were as fluid as life itself, all curves and implied movement. He removed the angles from the surface of the stone, allowing the smooth curves beneath to reveal themselves.

Which geometry was more native to the stone? The natural curve of atomic motion or the angularity of crystalline structure? Maybe both. If light can be both a particle and a wave, maybe art can be defined by both curve and angle.

Literature, too. The writer may not be a Michelangelo, but the process is essentially the same—chiseling, shaping, polishing until the awkward angles of the prose become smooth, fluid.

But no matter how polished the finished work, the writer isn't likely to make a name the way Homer did—by memorizing the text and spouting it out for anyone who'll listen.

Writers need editors and publishers. Not only that, they also need marketing directors, cover designers, typesetters, copyeditors, and distributors. Even the best writers need help beyond the page.

I've known some writers who've tried to go it alone. One convinced the local Walmart to let him set up a table in the front of the store and hawk his homemade book to passersby. Another urged all his friends to buy a copy of his self-published book on one particular day so it would register as a blip on Amazon's best-seller list and perhaps generate a steady stream of sales through a sort of lemming effect. But neither of these approaches worked. Writers need a good press behind them. Period.

In recent years, however, fewer and fewer big presses seem to be interested in writers. The major New York houses used to publish many of the so-called mid-list writers—those who write what is often regarded as serious literary fiction, the kind that gets nominated for Pulitzer Prizes and National Book Awards. Sure, those places will still issue brand-name genre books—murder mysteries by famous authors, and sci-fi, and romance, and all the other niche categories that thrive in the marketplace. They'll also be happy to publish your diet book or your collection of Cajun recipes. But a solid literary book by a new author is a hard sell in the corporate boardrooms these days.

Even successful veterans of the business are having trouble. I know a Pulitzer Prize recipient who couldn't get anyone interested in his new manuscript and decided to go straight to self-published e-book. I recently got a rejection from a head editor at a major publishing house who claimed that he loved my manuscript, but his desire to publish it had been overruled by someone in the marketing department, who didn't like its projected profit margin. The quality-driven world in which previous generations of writers operated is gone.

Happily, a new world has risen to take its place. Small presses have stepped in to fill the literary gap. We're now publishing more writers than ever in this country. Better ones, too. The landscape is different, of course. Instead of six publishing houses selling ten million books to American consumers, we have a few hundred presses selling a few thousand books each. No voice dominates, but many voices can now be heard.

Some small presses are run by long-time editors who won their spurs at the big houses, while others are mom-and-pop start-up operations run by people who simply love good literature. But perhaps the most important of all these small presses is the type that defines itself through its teaching. A teaching press, one affiliated with a university and that allows students to participate in the publishing process, preserves the business of publishing as a grass-roots enterprise and helps ensure the survival of literary publishing into the next generation. Such presses operate more on idealism than on profit margins, which is to say that the quality of a manuscript trumps its ultimate marketability.

New Rivers Press is such an operation. As a writer, I found it energizing to work with student editors, partly because they were possessed of an unjaded enthusiasm, and partly because there was much they didn't understand. When they raised questions about my manuscript, I had to clearly explain and justify my choices, and that forced me to rethink some of the decisions I'd made. In several cases, I found that their take on an issue was superior to my own, and I revised accordingly. Thus, we ended up teaching each other. New Rivers always had true professionals waiting in the wings in case I needed them to resolve a difference of opinion (which never happened). But working with young people was healthy for me in that it gave me access to a different generational perspective. It was also refreshing to work with a crew whose careers weren't on the line, as is often the case in the cutthroat realm of New York publishing. I enjoyed working with a core of editors who weren't driven by fear and paranoia. The students just wanted my book to be good; their jobs didn't hinge on how many copies it sold. I never had to second-guess their angles.

In 1980, Louisiana State University Press made history when it became the first small university outfit to publish a Pulitzer Prize-winning novel (*A Confederacy of Dunces* by John Kennedy Toole). That was a sign of things to come. Inevitably, more and more small presses will steal the spotlight as more and more of our finest writers will find homes with the smaller houses.

Publishing is being reduced to its atomic level, in that regard. Small, well-rounded operations are creating the new building blocks of a literate society—and that's fine with me. I don't mind that the giant corporations have veered away from the literary heartland. The books that survive our time may not bear the imprint of any of those major publishing conglomerates. The works that endure will be those published not for money but for love of literature. That's why I believe in New Rivers. They're ahead of the curve. That's their angle.

ROBERT ALEXANDER

Robert Alexander is a long-time friend of small press publishing and New Rivers Press in particular, where for many years he served in various capacities as contributing editor, creative director, member of the board of directors, and friend to Bill Truesdale.

Dear Friends,

I have a recurring dream. I'm standing in the parking lot of the Ford Centre in Minneapolis—built strong enough to take the weight of a Model T assembly line—about to enter the building and ride the elevator to the New Rivers office along with the daily crowd of artists and freelancers off to their own cubicles. It's another fall day in the Cities and there are yellow leaves on the trees, a touch of cool air on my face. It occurs to me suddenly that Bill has asked me to write a fund-raising paragraph for the new catalog, and today is the day we are putting the finishing touches on it before it goes off to the printer. But I've completely forgotten about it, and I have nothing, nothing to show him. I've come all the way up from Madison and I'm standing there without any pants on. And even in my suitcase back at the hotel I have nothing, no pants to cover my boxer shorts as I enter the building carrying a yellow pad with no writing on it, and stand in the elevator with all the artists gawking at me. In the hallway on the ninth floor there's the New Rivers door in front of me, and I look down and still no pants, no writing on the yellow pad, and the air from the open doorway is cold on my bare legs . . .

and then I'm awake, having thrown the blankets off and the wind through the window I've left open the night before, a light breeze still summery and pleasant, the wind has shifted, and blowing now cold from the northwest has swept my yellow pad from the bedside table and damn it's cold on my bare legs. And then I remember: New Rivers has left the old Ford Centre forever—and Bill is dead. And my yellow pad is still blank, the essay I was intending to write for this book forgotten in the busyness of my life. But still, but still, dear friends, New Rivers is putting forth, each publishing season, several delectable items of fiction and poetry, the best of new and emerging authors from the Midwest and beyond. And knowing that, I can get up this morning and, in anticipation of New Rivers Press's 50th birthday, put one more pot of coffee on the stove.

—Robert Alexander